I0840854

Friends

Two-Legs, Four-Legs, Six-Legs, Wings and Roots

by
The Lonesome Hillbilly

Books by the same author

The Book on Motorcycle Camping
How to Live on the Road Full Time

Places: I'm Going to Go Back There, Some Day

Roads: All Roads Lead to Roam

Friends: Two-Legs, Four-Legs, Six-Legs, Wings and Roots

Visions: Things and Ideas Found in the Wild

Elements: Elemental, Elementary

Things in Heaven and Earth
Essays from Places, Roads, Friends, Visions and Elements
with full-color illustrations

Dedicated to
All of my Friends,
Especially those who have been there
Whether I needed them or not.
You know who you are.

CONTENTS

The Friends
1927
by Rudyard Kipling

I had some friends—but I dreamed that they were dead—
Who used to dance with lanterns round a little boy in bed;
Green and white lanterns that waved to and fro:
But I haven't seen a Firefly since ever so long ago!

I had some friends—their crowns were in the sky—
Who used to nod and whisper when a little boy went by,
As the nuts began to tumble and the breeze began to blow:
And I haven't seen a Cocoa-palm since ever so long ago!

I had a friend—he came up from Cape Horn,
With a Coal-sack on his shoulder when a little boy was born.
He heard me learn to talk, and he helped me thrive and grow:
But I haven't seen the Southern Cross since ever so long ago!

I had a boat—I out and let her drive,
Till I found my dream was foolish, for my friends were all
    alive.
The Cocoa-palms were real, and the Southern Cross was true:
And the Fireflies were dancing—so I danced too!

Introduction:
Pathos

There is a useful concept in the scientific world called The Pathetic Fallacy. It is from the Greek word "pathos", the root of the words "sympathy" and "empathy". Today "pathetic" is commonly used to mean "pitifully bad", but in this case, has no negative connotation; it simply means "feeling". The Pathetic Fallacy is the error of attributing human ideas, goals, needs, *feelings*, to non-human things. Examples are "water wants to flow downhill", "trees want to reach up to the light", and "a bear sow wants to protect her cubs". Some will say the bear sow is only acting out of instinct, that there is no emotion there. I doubt that strongly, but until we learn to speak Bearish, we will likely never know with certainty. Certainly most trees will survive better if they gain access to stronger and more intense light, but does it have any desire to do so? That would require some form or degree of consciousness, of will. No degreed scientist that I am aware of has ever determined whether trees have consciousness or not, or is willing to admit to such a determination. (I have seen such evidence, but as I have no degree, I am an "unqualified observer". Shows you how much *they* know.) As to water, there are very few people who would maintain that any body of water has any degree of awareness by any definition (except the men who live on the sea; they know). On the other hand, there is no *proof* one way or the other. Not that anyone has looked for any; it would be a career-ender for any doctoral candidate to even propose such a thesis.

Still, I often employ the Pathetic Fallacy, writing of voices in the water, and thoughts of trees, and conversations with squirrels. Why? Because it works. It makes a point. Much of what we see in Nature and in the rest of the world is only reflections of our selves. Just as we need a mirror to see the features of our own faces, so do we need a reflector to see the depths of our souls, or minds, or selves, whatever term suits you. "Know thyself" is the single most important philosophical principle, for to the degree that you understand yourself, all other knowledge becomes more valuable, more applicable. An old army maxim states "If it's stupid and it works, it ain't stupid". Fine. If a fallacious observation causes one person to think, to come to a new realization, it is valid, not fallacious.

Another factor is the concept of "oneness with Nature". This can mean many different things to different people, from silly superstition to incontestable fact. I do not know what various people conceive this to be, and I do not really care, for it is not germane. What *I* mean when I speak it, what I am trying to communicate, is that I am a part of Nature. My body (not *me*, the spirit, but my material body) is an animal, just as a bear or a beaver, and it is a part of the universe, just as a rock or a rainstorm. I am a part, a piece, a segment of Nature and of the Universe. Destroy me, and Nature is somewhat the less for it. Thus, I am one with Nature. And equally, thus, damage any part of Nature and you damage me. And again, thus, I feel that I am, from a certain viewpoint, *all* of Nature.

And this leads to the broad viewpoint. I feel sympathy for the deer brought down by the puma. I feel its pain. I feel empathy for the puma. I feel its satisfaction, its well-being from having gained food for the next few days. The grass traps the sunlight, the deer slaughters the grass, the puma devours the deer, and eventually the grass feeds on the puma. There is pain and pleasure, destruction and construction, death and birth, but the important factor is that there is balance. Over time, everything gives as much as it takes, there is exactly as much destruction as construction. I see this in the human race, in predator and prey, in forest and wildfire. I see it as a reflection of myself. Pathetic Fallacy, but in this case, no fallacy at all.

The true Pathetic Fallacy lies not in the seeing of human traits in non-human subjects, for the traits are often there in fact. The fallacy lies in assuming that the traits are never there. Water does not flow downhill because it wants to, but because it must. Gravity requires it. But this is not proof that water does not have the desire. Granted, such a desire is very, *very* unlikely, but there is no proof of its absence. Assuming the absence and refusing to even consider that there is any possibility of its existence, *that* is pathetic.

Two-Legs

Stereotypes

Stereotyping is a risky action. It means to look at a person or a thing and, based on obvious surface appearances, to put that person or thing into a category and assume that all of the details will fit. In the Old West, it was a common thing to come across a drifting cowhand, who rode up to a trail herd or a ranch line camp looking for work. Clearly just another no-account saddle tramp. But that night at the campfire, you learn he was educated at Oxford, and he ends up trading poetry with the camp cook, who was a successful lawyer in New York City before he became bored with the lifestyle and headed west. Stereotyping is risky, but it exists for a reason: The originals do exist, perfectly true to the type. If you meet enough people, you will find them; they are not uncommon at all. Pointing it out may be offensive, especially to a Dumb Blonde or a Macho Bully; they hate being labelled, the more so because the label fits. It also offends the Newspeakers, the fools who push Political Correctness, who abhor direct speech and words that have precise and correct meanings. If you are such a (ahem) person, prepare to be offended. I have met several stereotypes in my sojourn in the Cities, and meet many more in the course of my travels. I want to stress here that all of these descriptions are factual, and I have not exaggerated or enhanced anything. This is all true and accurate.

For example, every movie-goer knows The Busy Big Businessman and his Beautiful Sharp Female Executive Assistant. He is talking on two phones (minimum) at once, bartering garment import quotas in units of a million dozen, snapping three- or four-word orders to the Assistant, who relays the orders in fully detailed paragraphs to office workers who scurry to comply. He is a New Yorker, she is Chinese. This is straight out of Hollywood. I *know* truth is stranger than fiction, for that is exactly where I met them, while designing a system to computerize their dealings, and I have not invented, altered or stretched a single datum. They truly did deal in million dozens. And made a *lot* of money.

About the same time, I met the Paranoid Entrepeneur, also computerizing his business. He had the Great Idea that would make him a millionaire overnight, but was deathly afraid someone would steal it. It had to do with comparison of RV features, but I cannot give any details, because he insisted I sign a half-million dollar bond to not reveal his secrets. He printed his datasheets in red-brown ink on deep red paper so they could not be photocopied; they could hardly be read. The data he gave me to write the program was inaccurate; once the program was written, he would replace them with true data.

It was in the early seventies when I set out from Massachusetts, walking, backpacking, with no particular destination, even in mind. My only plan was to roam the National Forests, to camp out, to be in the wilder lands. I was going west and south, only because if I went east or north, I would quickly run out of land. After a few months I wandered into Missouri, into the Ozark Mountains, near Lake of the Ozarks. It was mostly open hills at the time, many villages and small settlements, but plenty of undeveloped back-country and miles of undisturbed lakeshore. I came upon an old cabin, an unpainted shack, grey and weathered, with a rickety covered porch. In front of the porch there were a few coon hounds, lazily watching me, ready to bark if I approached, but willing to just lie there if I only passed by. On the porch were four rocking chairs, each occupied by a grey-headed old-timer in patched and faded blue jeans. They were passing a stone jug of moonshine. Pa Kettle and cronies in Dogpatch, exactly as Hollywood would portray them, or the Hee-Haw Lazy Porch, except (durn it!) without the girls in short-shorts and tight tops. They called me over and invited me to "set a spell an' rest yore feet". They passed me the jug, smooth and explosive; each dog thumped his tail, twice. They asked me where I was from. I told them, and they said they was glad to hear it, mighty glad. Walked from Massachusetts? Young folk don' do that kinda thing no more, they rahd their otty-mobeels an' won't hardly walk two miles at a stretch. 'Tain't lahk th' old days atall. They declared me an Honorary Hillbilly, and named me The Lonesome Hillbilly; it has been my road name ever since. You likely don't believe me. You think I made it up, or at least stretched it some. Well, maybe stretched; maybe one of the hounds did thump his tail more than twice. But it is true: I met the solid stereotype, and was given the name.

Just yesterday, in Tourist Country, I entered the local hardware store looking for 3-in-1 and linseed oil. There were nuts and bolts, nails and screws, RV water fittings and toilet parts, solvents and motor oils, four colors of paint, even linseed oil and WD-40, but no 3-in-1 oil. The proprietor was a comely woman, mid-thirties. She was breaking in a new clerk, a twenty year old blonde girl, built like a brick - - - ah, composting toilet.

"So", the proprietor said, "you need to know about plumbing parts, male and female. The female part is bigger, and they fit together, the male part fits into the female part."

"One part goes inside the other?"

"Yes, like a pipe into a connector, then they are brazed together."

"Brazed?"

"Like welding."

"Oh. So the pipe goes inside the connector. The pipe is the male part and --- Oh! Tee-hee!"

I'm sure if I got to know her better, she would turn out to not be particularly dumb. Maybe.

I told the proprietor I was looking for 3-in-1 oil, and asked if she carried it. "3-in-1? What's that?" I explained. "No, I don't. In eight years running the store, I never heard of it." Really, that is what she said. I told her it was okay, at least she had linseed oil. "Oh, will that do instead?"

Well, it is Tourist Country, with every bit of the economy geared to ripping --- sorry, I mean servicing the needs of tourists. But finding the Woman in a Hardware Store *and* the Dumb Blonde in the same room --- I was tempted to ask for a hole-puller or a left-handed paintbrush. Fortunately, I did not. As I said, stereotyping can be risky.

A common stereotype is the City Boy Who Thinks He is Camping. He pulls up in a sixty foot motor home, with a full kitchen including refrigerator, freezer and microwave, a full bathroom with shower and hot water, bedroom, dining room, 56" television with a DVD player and a satellite dish, and he is just as proud of it as a dog who has just rolled in three-day-old skunk roadkill. He carries fifteen sets of clean clothing per person, so they can don fresh stuff every morning, and shower and change for the evening after a hard day visiting the park gift shops and IMAX theater. He has to have all of these clean clothes because he is roughing it; the motor home does not have a clothes washer or a dryer. It does have a dishwasher, though. He also has to visit a dump station every three days to empty the waste-water tank; more roughing it. And he only brought three neckties!

And then you have the Efficiency Expert On Vacation. I found him in Yellowstone National Park. His wife and children were heading off to See the Sights, and he was admonishing them to be sure to be back by three, because they had a Schedule to Keep. Yes, he had an itinerary, an *hourly* itinerary, for their entire two-week vacation, and they were by George going to stick to it! When he got back home, he would have Been There, and would have the photographs to prove it. He was completely oblivious to the fact that that was *all* he would have;the idea of having fun, of actually enjoying the vacation, clearly had never occurred to him. But then, he probably would not have understood it.

The Campfire Duffer is actually quite common; many of you have seen him, even in city parks. He starts his fire at dusk, a good hour later than he should. He piles the wood in the Official Tepee form which he has learned from the movies, pours on the fire starter, and burns his eyebrows off. Roaring flames leap six feet in the air, the heat driving him ten feet back. They dance and glow and slowly die back, leaving a charred pyramid of blackened smoking wood. Green wood. Not split. With the bark still on. If he is a Stubborn Duffer, he will persist. He may toss in another cup of fire starter, or if he is stupid, squirt it on, explode the can, and get hauled off to get his massive second-degree burns treated. He will stuff paper under the wood, and pine cones and leaves and dirt. Eventually he may get some wood burning, and settle for small flames and a massive smoke plume. Well, he got the fire started, didn't he? And he will then complain about how the smoke follows him around wherever he moves, and wonder how the counsellors at Camp Winnekahootchie did it.

We also find the Old Mountain Man. Long gray beard, long gray hair, weathered face and hands, eyes narrowed by the sun (for he *never* wears sunglasses), dressed in denim or leather or khaki canvas, long knife on his belt, and maybe a pistol, and a long, stout walking staff. Boots or moccasins. Leather jacket with fringes, many of them missing. Wide-brimmed hat, or a fur cap made from the hide of a small animal, often with the tail and maybe the head still attached. Knows every tree by name, and can start a fire by giving the wood a hard look. Never found in cities, and not often in campgrounds or National Parks. I am often mistaken for one, as I have the superficial appearance, but the real Old Mountain Man knows everything there is to know about mountains and forests, and then some, and can track a rabbit across a parking lot, or a hawk through the air; I can't. (The Old Desert Rat looks exactly the same, only browner, and knows the deserts instead of the mountains.)

You will certainly find The Biker here as well; he is ubiquitous. Not the Tough Biker or the Outlaw Biker, just (dramatic drumbeats) The Biker. One look at him and you know he is ready to stomp your ribs in at the slightest offense. He is Big, well-muscled, deeply bronzed, tattoos on biceps, wearing black leather boots, pants and vest (shirt optional), no helmet on his bald head, unless the law requires it, and then it is the smallest one he can get. Also black. Shiny chains and metal ornaments on the vest. Sticker or decal on the windshield that says "Shit better *not* happen!" That is the stereotype, right out of Hollywood. He does exist, but is actually quite rare. The Real Thing has the same physical appearance, but under it there is a human being. If you get into trouble or need help, no one will be more ready to lend a hand than a biker. Even a Hell's Angel.

A scientist once did a study of an inbred family, and called them the Kalikaks. Their primary characteristic was that they were very deficient mentally, so much so that they thought they were normal. I met some in a campground. They looked just as one would expect, with identical vacant expressions, clearly similar features, slow moving and even slower thinking, grossly overweight, and blissfully unaware of any flaws. The fifteen-year-old daughter tried to flirt with me, clearly thinking she was attractive. They had strong local accents, so strong I could place their home within a hundred miles. I will not divulge it, because most of the people there are quite intelligent, but the stereotype always includes a strong accent, usually country or inner-city. They were actually quite hilarious, but that is another story.

There are many, many more: The Great Chef Who Cannot Cook, the Honest Politician You Would Not Buy a Skateboard From, the Health Food Dietician Who is Half Dead, and so on. Most of them are pretty derogatory.

Most of the people I meet are not stereotypes. Generally they have a few of the characteristics, but nothing else matches. Much like me being mistaken for the Old Mountain Man. Even the ones I do meet I very quickly find they have greater depths. The Old Hillbillies were wells of wisdom, of practical knowledge about life and living in the outdoors. Why, I learned more in that afternoon than I had in the three months it took me to get there! Keep this in mind when you meet a Stereotype, a Typical Anything. You are probably misjudging a sensible, complex person.

But when you are right about them, it is truly memorable.

The Kalikaks

In my youth, I had read about the inbred Kalikak family, but I had never met any. Not until the day before yesterday, when a whole family of them set up in the campsite next to mine. Forty years ago I would have been amazed, but since then I have met so many solid stereotypes, now I just recognize them and add them to my collection. For those who are not familiar with the type, back in the mid-twentieth century a scientist did a study of an inbred family, tracing them back to the Revolutionary War, and made up the surname Kalikak to label them. They were singularly unintelligent, and had no idea at all that they were anything other than normal.

My neighbors were a family of five. They arrived in a small car, not a compact, but a four-door sedan. It would seat five, but could not have been comfortable, because they were all, except the father, quite large people. The trunk was full, tightly packed, and there was gear lashed to the roof. There was more gear, notably a cooler of food, that was not lashed on. Not by the time they arrived. After everything had been unpacked, one of them noticed the absence. Where is the cooler? Did we leave it at home? No, I packed it. On the top. Where is it? It ain't here. You sure you packed it? Yeah, I'm sure. Where is it? Must have fallen off. Where is the canopy? Did we leave it at home? No, I packed it. (Note: I have omitted the bad words. About a third of the total count.)

Seems to me it should be somewhat difficult to not notice such things falling off.

The mother was enormously fat, and the father skeletally skinny. She could barely walk, just sort of shuffled, her feet almost never leaving the ground. He, oddly enough, had much the same walk. She would get tired from walking ten feet; he seemed to tire out from sitting, tired all of the time; his head was permanently bowed, and never raised above forty-five degrees. I suspect he was chronically worn out from working all of the time. Probably held two full-time jobs, just to support the family. From overheard remarks, I learned the wife did not have any job, not even making craftswork to sell. She had red-brown hair, with half-inch long gray roots; his hair was all gray. Aside from that, they were virtually identical, the same features, the same mannerisms. They could easily have been brother and sister, or at least first cousins. They very probably were. The children also bore the same features. I do not mean they had the expected family resemblance; I mean they were as similar as twins.

The elder son, about eighteen, was even fatter than his mother; he had boobs, about a C cup. (Yes, I know the term is politically incorrect, which is fine with me, and if it offends you, you deserve it. Besides, the pun is just so appropriate in this case. His father had boobs, too: A wife, two sons and a daughter.) When walking, the boy would pause every seven or eight steps to rest for a few seconds. The only walking (if such a shuffle can be dignified with the term "walking") I ever saw him do was to the outhouse and back. Otherwise he sat in his chair from waking to bedtime. Well, not quite: He would get up to get food. I expect he got more exercise getting food than he did in his twice-daily toilet breaks. (The whole family ducked behind their tent to urinate. One at a time.)

The younger son and the daughter looked somewhere between fourteen and sixteen. While not as fat as their mother, they were quite large, waddled the same way, and almost never stood. On their faces, they had the same vacant expression as their brother; their mouths were rarely completely closed, and their eyes only half open. The daughter's voice was very high-pitched, about what one might expect from an eight-year-old, and whiny. Most of what little she said was complaints, about how nothing was right, and how everyone treated her badly. Most of her talking was done while cooking, or rather, while standing over food on the fire. I am not sure I can call it cooking, because she complained that she could not tell if anything was done, or keep the fire burning, and her younger brother had to come check it, and tend the fire. Not that he could keep it burning either, but he could make it produce a lot more smoke.

I cannot comment much on their conversation, because they did not have much available for comment. The older son did almost all of the talking. He would make a remark and repeat it, unvaried, not a single word added, omitted or out of place, three or four times. He would pause for ten or fifteen seconds, then repeat again. Often there was a third cycle, and possibly even a fourth one. Then he would come up with a new remark, and run it through the same routine. All day, he would continue. Except when toiling to the outhouse, when he saved his breath. Sometimes one of the prior remarks would reappear for a rerun. Now and then he would remain silent for a whole minute, maybe even two. On occasion, after about a half-hour, maybe an hour, his mother would make a short comment, which would cut his cycle short and start him on a new one. Maybe a dozen times a day the younger siblings would join in, but they generally only talked to each other, she complaining about something such as not being able to tell if the food was done, he telling her she was not any good at whatever she was doing, but that everyone loved her, especially him, so do not get upset, and the food is done. Then the elder brother began droning again. And in all of this, I do not recall anyone ever uttering even a single sentence that did not contain at least one obscenity or profanity. Not even just to say "yes". Except the father. He never uttered a word.

No one talked at all during meals.

Now, the usual stereotype for such an idiocratic family requires a dozen or so offspring, but this one had only the three. I theorize that either the father's potency broke down from overwork, or else, more likely, there were a dozen or so other children who had already grown up and gone off on their own. At any rate, they are not new to camping. They are . . . not *skilled*; no, that is not the correct word. Experienced? Familiar? Practiced? They have clearly done this before. They set up their tent (on uneven ground) quickly, though the guys were not placed well or out of the way. They started their fires the same way every time, with too much lighting fluid, but knew enough to not add more after lighting the fire. Probably lost a sibling, or more likely two or three, that way. They had an accustomed pattern for laying out their chairs. They even bought seasoned wood for the campfire. But they also persisted in trying to get green wood to burn. They were quite stubborn about it. They never gave up, and never could figure out why it would not burn.

Life is full of little desironies (those are good ironies, desirable ironies). The Kalikaks were undoubtedly the worst campers I have ever seen, and the most blithely unaware of their shortcomings. I have often tolerantly poked fun at, shall we say, less-than-skilled campers, because I can identify with them, having once been just as ignorant and having made many of the same mistakes they make. But not the Kalikaks. They were so consummately foolish, even stupid, I could find no common ground with them at all. So, while their presence was amusing, in the same way a spectacularly bad movie can be entertaining, I was pleased to see them go. And even more pleased when, less than an hour later, their site was occupied by a new couple, recently retired, in their new eighteen foot trailer. Though only on their second camping trip, they seem to have almost everything they need, and very little that they do not. They know, fairly well, what they are doing, and are well aware that there is a lot yet to learn. I do not know if they understand yet that there will always be a lot left to learn. I always appreciate sensible people, and much more so now, with so recent an example of the Dark Side for comparison. I have recognized these new folk as gold friends. We shall have a fine time for the next couple of days!

Weekend Wanderers

Coyote Creek, one of the New Mexico State Parks, ranks among the best and worst campgrounds I have ever seen. That is because there are essentially two separate campgrounds. The good one is up the hill. Picnic tables and fire rings at every site, water and vault toilets (outhouses) nearby. Not too far away is a bathhouse with flush toilets and sinks and a pair of shower stalls. Here are also electric outlets where you can charge your electronics, and a wifi transceiver that is somewhat erratic, but it works well enough if you are patient. The campsites are set among trees, so the area is shady (though it never gets really hot, rarely as much as 90). There are a couple of good hiking trails through beautiful, thick woods. The area only gets about eighteen inches of rain each year, but the growth is very verdant in spite of that. The fishing, or at least the catching, is *very* good, as Coyote Creek is the most heavily stocked trout stream in New Mexico.

The other campground is right next to the bathhouse. There are a eight or ten tent sites scattered around, all but two of them with fire rings. Those two are next to the propane tank for heating the shower water; not a wise idea to have fires there. But the main part is the sites with water and electricity hook-ups. Ten sites, each with a power box, and one waterpoint for each two sites. Each site has a parking area twenty feet square, which limits the size of RV supported. Then another twenty feet to a picnic table, and a fire ring beyond it, all on a large grassy meadow. Sounds nice, doesn't it? But the sites butt up against each other. Not one inch of space between them. Ten sites crammed into a straight, two hundred foot row. When it is full, it *feels* full, it is *crowded*. Most of the occupants have their dogs, and twenty feet is too small a personal space for many of them. They bark. They whine. They annoy. The larger dogs are usually okay. They pretty much ignore the little yappers as beneath their dignity. But some of the little sons and daughters of bitches have no grasp of reality. Dogs are naturally superstitious. Every dog knows with fanatic fervor that any dog, be it ever so small, can beat any other dog, however large and fierce, if the little dog is in his own yard. One little nuisance, who did not stand ten inches tall, was left behind, in a cage, while his people went off to do something. He yapped, non-stop, for three solid hours.

Often these campers bring along a clutch of small children, say, under twelve years old. They do not go off to the playground that is set between the two campgrounds, and equipped with slides and swings and such gear. They go into the grassy meadow and play their games there, games played with sticks and rocks and whatever they can find. As you may recall from your own childhood (I certainly do), these made-up games are always more fun than anything the adults designed. If *I* were building a playground, I would make it part hill, part flat, mostly grassy but with a large part just sand. I would provide playground equipment: Large boxes of sticks and many sizes of wooden blocks, big cardboard boxes that kids can turn into trucks or tanks or houses, or use to slide downhill, and a big pile of small sandbags, small enough for a six-year-old to carry. Bet the kids would love it. But my point is, these kids do not play quietly. They yell and scream and laugh and shout as they run around and chase each other. They are louder than the dogs, and even more persistent. So why is their noise pleasing, while that of the dogs is not? Why do I sit and listen to them, watching their antics, sharing their laughter, and holding this to be a high point of the day, and why do I sit, annoyed by the dog's yapping, dreaming of how satisfying it would be to shoot the little bugger?

I needed a week of electricity and internet access to work on my writing, so I was stuck with one of these Levittown sites. It was fine all the way through Friday afternoon. Then the weekenders arrived. These are the folks who have nine-to-five Monday-to-Friday jobs. They leave home as early as they can, and pull into the campground late, sometimes after dark. Their rig has to be braced and leveled, plugged in and connected to the water-point. Then they can turn in and rest up from their journey. Some will sleep late in the morning, some will rise with the sun. After breakfast they are off to do their hiking and fishing and whatever, cramming as much fun into the day as they can, poor souls. They have to rush, because they have such a short time. But some just drag out a chair and sit in the sun or shade and relax and enjoy being here. Either way, it is good. It is their vacation, to enjoy as they see fit.

On Saturday morning, early or late, others arrive, others who live too far away to get here in one evening. Mostly they leave early, three or four AM, with the intent of arriving sometime before noon. They will set up, and relax or get busy, as they choose. Regardless of having arrived many hours later than the first group, these will be leaving about the same time, between noon and two PM on Sunday. Almost all campgrounds have a two PM "checkout" time, and many will stay right to the limit, cramming in every minute they can. They value their camping; it is rare, and scarce, for it is very limited. For all of their labor and expense in getting here (and getting back), they get one day, at most a day and a half, of play. Those few hours are expensive, and precious. They will not squander a single minute if they can avoid it.

So why is it, Sunday morning, almost three quarters of them are packing up? It is only six AM, but the husbands are disengaging the levelers, while the wives and kids are dismantling their gear and packing up their food and tools? I ask them, and they complain of the weather. It rained last night, and the weather report calls for rain all morning. Well, it is late July, and that means monsoon season. But the afternoon is likely to be mostly clear. Would it not be better for driving if they waited? And they reply, they do not want to just sit inside all morning. There is nothing to do when it is raining.

Nothing to do.

I leave them to their packing. I eat some breakfast and don my gear, then set out for the woods. I listen to the rain pattering in the leaves and needles, watch the spreading circles of drops in the creek, peer into the water to follow the muddy swirls introduced by the runnels of run-off draining from the banks. Tiny fry swarm among the clouds, snapping up snacks invisible to me. Minnows dart through to devour the fry, and grown trout ambush the minnows. On a clear day there is little activity to be seen. The fry hide among the pebbles, and the trout sit in the deeper water waiting for a dollop of food to drift by. There is none of this frenetic rush to take advantage of the rain's largesse, for food is apparantly only abundant when the water is roiled and rising. I spend half of the morning here, where the rain is broken by the trees; I hardly need any rain gear at all. And when the rain ends, there is a magnificent rainbow, one end touching down on an outhouse. So much for the pot of gold.

When I return to camp, there are only three sites still occupied, two of us in tents. There are three empty sites on either side of me. I have space. I have had a wonderful time, the rain has stopped, and it is not yet ten o'clock. There will likely be occasional showers for the rest of the day, but mostly not. For now, the air is damp, the scents intense, and birds are chattering away. The robins are having a feast, snapping up worms and bugs flooded out of hiding by the rain. The day is gorgeous, and nothing is wrong. It is a great pity that so many people are missing it.

Such a Tiny Tent

I see people arriving in forty-, fifty-, sixty-foot motor homes and fifth-wheel trailers. Almost always, it serves only two people. Sometimes a family with two, three, or four kids. Sometimes a single person. For many, it is their home. For most, it is a vacation vehicle. And they own it. Rental RVs are almost always much smaller. There are a few people who use a small trailer, a pop-up or a Li'l Snoozy, twelve or fifteen feet long, or a camper in the bed of a pickup truck. But they are a small percentage. There are more who have no trailer at all. They use a tent.

Now, commercial tents are small. Even the big ones are small. They are rated by sleeping capacity, and apparently the standard is six feet by two feet per person. A three-man tent is six or seven feet square, and has plenty of headroom for a person to sit upright. The smallest I have seen which allows a person to stand upright was eight by ten, with six feet of headroom. It was rated as a six-man tent. That means six people can crowd into it, leaving no room for gear. My canvas tent is eight by ten. I would rate it as big enough for two people, plus their gear. It is also bulky; it would take four or five commercial tents to equal its bulk. However, bulk and weight really only matter to backpackers and horsemen (excuse me, equestrians), and bikers (bicycle and motorcycle). Those who go camping in a car can easily afford to carry a large tent. So why do ninety-five percent of them buy the minimum size?

The young couples have a nice three-man tent. They are probably sharing a double sleeping bag, so there is plenty of floor space. Well, maybe just enough, if they include a bag for clothing. And most of their gear can be left in the car, out of the weather. But when they get dressed, or change clothes, they have to do it sitting down, or kneeling, or crouched over. Why not get a six-man tent? The three-man costs forty dollars, the six-man costs seventy. I would think the comfort and convenience would be worth thirty dollars, especially if you run into a rainy day or two. (I once spent two rainy days in a three-man tent, and immediately upgraded to a six-man.) Or if the mosquitos are particularly bad, and you want a place where you can eat in peace. Call me a sybarite or a hedonist or a wimp, if it pleases you, but I like to be comfortable when I am camping. It is an awful lot more fun. I am not talking about luxury, just being able to roll over without waking someone up.

Here is a party who just pulled in across from me. Four adults and two small children. I saw a similar camp, same assortment of people, last year. They pitched two six-man tents, one for each couple, and a three-man for the kids. I saw a family with three kids, who set up a six-man for the parents. Each child had a personal kiddie tent, a pink dome with a fairy-tale castle painted on it, a conical tepee, and an army-style pup tent. That is doing it right! But the family across the way? One six-man tent for all six of them.

I think these people believe marketing. I suspect they feel there is something wrong, sinful, *wasteful* about using a larger tent. The couple uses a three-man tent because they could not find a two-man. (I was actually told that very thing by one young man.) And back when I used a six-man dome tent, several people told me it was way too big for just one person. Oddly enough, no one has yet made any disparaging comments about the size of my canvas tent, even though it is larger than the old six-man. Perhaps because I made it myself, so it lacks a manufacturer's size rating. Or, more precisely, the manufacturer (me) rated it as a one-man tent.

I have never known a biker who camped in anything larger than a three-man tent, except a couple who upgraded after seeing my six-man, and two who had trailers that folded out into tents. I have known a few people who lived in a van or station wagon, who were puzzled by those who seemed to need a fifty- or sixty-foot RV for only two occupants, but most people think it not unreasonable at all. But very few see anything odd in car campers using such tiny tents. Maybe they are thinking of Harry Potter or Magical Mystery Tour.

One of the great attractions of camping, of the outdoor lifestyle, is the wide open spaces, plains stretching to a distant horizon, mountains from which you can see a hundred miles, unlimited dark skies full of stars that lie dozens of light-years away, or more. It just does not make any sense to huddle inside a cramped tiny tent when you can so easily afford a roomy and comfortable one. Does it not?

Setting Up

It is always interesting, in campgrounds, to watch the new arrivals. There are backpackers and bicyclists, motorcycle and car tenters, vans and pickup-bed campers, trailers and fifth-wheels, and full motor-homes, small and large. However they travel, they all, with very few exceptions, must set up their camp. The experienced ones, the ones with years of practice, naturally accomplish the task the most quickly. The newbies on their first or second trip take substantially longer.

The exceptions are the rare ones in vans or station wagons who do no setup, for they carry almost no gear. I know of one who lives in a station wagon. He has built in a bed (with no headroom) with drawers underneath. He lets down the tailgate to serve as a table for cooking. He has to climb on the bed to access his clothes and books and such, but the only things he actually unpacks are a folding chair and a TV table. He arrives in camp and is set up within two minutes, and half of that time is getting out of the car and stretching.

Everyone else takes a bit longer. The backpackers and the bicyclists usually sit and rest for a few minutes, easing their shoulders and legs, then set to work. First the tent is unpacked and pitched after preparing the ground, picking a suitable spot with no roots or humps, and removing any rocks or branches that would make uncomfortable lumps. Then the cooking gear is laid out, ready for dinner, sleeping bags unrolled, and the rest of the gear stowed in the tent to be safe from rain or heavy dew. It takes about half an hour, maybe forty-five minutes.

The tenters ride in on their bike or in their car, then do much the same thing, pitching the tent and laying out the gear. The ones in cars leave a lot of their gear in the car, but they are also carrying more stuff, so laying out that which they will immediately use takes about the same time. Bikers with hard saddlebags will leave gear in them, others with soft (not rain-proof) bags will toss the bags into the tent. It still takes about half an hour, maybe forty-five minutes.

The ones in vans and pickup-bed campers have a clear advantage: No tent to pitch. But they usually set up a canopy, and they always have gear to move out, to get it off of the bed and out of the way so they can move around inside their vehicle. It takes about half an hour, maybe forty-five minutes.

The pop-up trailers take more work. The campers have to set up leveling jacks, then crank the roof up, by hand or by motor. The cloth sides need to be attached, and usually have stiffeners to be installed. But once that is done, all that is left is to bring out the camp chairs, so the entire setup only takes them about half an hour, maybe forty-five minutes.

The trailers and fifth-wheels usually require a fair bit of maneuvering to get them in place, so they generally do not finish arriving until ten or fifteen minutes after first arriving. Then the trailer can be unhitched, levelers positioned and adjusted, and the sliders, half-rooms that extend from the sides, cranked out. Counting the time spent fitting the rig into the campsite, it takes about half an hour, maybe forty-five minutes.

The motor homes are the easiest of all, or should be. They are self-powered, self-contained, mobile apartments, with toilets and showers and kitchens and bedrooms and dining rooms, complete, with everything. Only very reluctantly do I admit that they are some sort of camping at all. Setting up involves parking in place, chocking the wheels, setting and adjusting the levelers, extending the sliders, and lowering the awning. Often they also hook the rig up to an electricity box, waterpoint, and sometimes a sewer connection. That should be all, but it is not. Motor homes have a lot of room to carry stuff, and the owners will pack them full. This is in compliance with Jensen's Law, a scientific principle which states that anything and everything, if not constrained by an outside influence, will expand to consume the resources available, and then some. This is why your income is never quite enough, however many raises you get, and why the hard drive on your computer, the closets in your house, your attic or garage storage space, your kitchen drawers, your motor home storage bins, and so on and on, are always filling up. This extra stuff has to be hauled out and set up: Chairs, tables, lights, satellite dish, solar panels. (Fifth-wheels and larger trailers also share this problem.) All told, it ends up taking half an hour, maybe forty-five minutes.

Of course, that half hour is pretty generic. Some folks, especially in some of the bigger rigs, can take a lot more time. Sometimes, if only doing an overnight stop, it takes much less. When I am doing an overnight in clear weather, with no need for a tent, my setup takes five minutes: Unroll the sleeping bag, set up the camp chair, and open a can of beans. On the other hand, if I arrive early on a very sunny day, I probably will not pitch the tent till almost sunset, when the tent site is shady. Of course, that does not change the actual amount of time spent in setting up.

I have read that the Roman soldiers would set up a full camp every night, digging a ditch around it, using the dirt to build a wall, driving defensive stakes into the wall, and then pitching their tents inside, and all of that setup would be done in half an hour. Maybe forty-five minutes.

The more things change . . .

Camping Through the Years

Forty years ago, and more, I camped in the simplest style. I walked, and all I owned was in my pack or pockets or paws. I learned to save weight by making many things do double duty; tincture of iodine to disinfect wounds and water, tobacco to comfort my soul and to combat mosquitos, a staff to support my body by day and my tent by night. The less I owned, the easier life was. I would wander through the woods and the hills, slowly, stopping often to bathe in the gentle light filtering through the leaves, or to wonder at a valley revelling between pompous hills, sometimes stopping early to stay a day or two by a mischievous brook, sometimes continuing into the night to eventually lie in a hidden meadow till the dawn. It was quiet, lonesome, and good.

Now and then I would stay in a campground, visiting campfires, sharing meals, comparing and recommending (and warning of) places we had been, and sometimes just being together, silently gazing into the fire. There were a few like me, walking. There were some on bicycles, and many in cars or pickups, some with camper shells on the back, and even a few with small trailers. There was, very rarely, a Winnebago or something of the sort. Almost everyone slept in a tent, usually of heavy canvas with solid steel poles, and cooked over a wood fire or a gasoline stove. Firewood was usually abundant, and rarely far away, so even those who cooked on a stove would sit beside a fire. Most campgrounds had outhouses (called "vault toilets" today), many had wells, some had piped water, and a few, near towns, even had (oh, blessed luxury!) hot showers.

Most campers had radios, but never a television, for there were no signals to receive in the mountains. We had no satellites, no satellite dishes, no cable. Just broadcast, and that requires line-of-sight for any reception at all.

Gear was simpler, for there was little available; campers were not a big market. Instead of freeze-dried food or just-add-water, we had cans, and sacks of flour or cornmeal. Likely the most common meal was a can of old Dinty Moore Beef Stew, lightly seasoned with Off! insect repellent, eaten from an Army surplus mess kit with a steel spoon.

Times have changed, as they always do. Camping is now Big Business. There are very light and roomy tents that are designed be pitched or struck in ten or fifteen minutes, and are well-ventilated and truly waterproof (some of them). There are hand-cranked LED flashlights and radios, modern sturdy and lightweight boots and packs, freeze-dried meals, effective water purifiers, solar panels, indeed, an awe-inspiring array of everything you need, and even more you do not need, for a memorable outdoor experience. Camping has been improved tremendously, and degraded even more.

Not for all of us, of course. There are still many who hike, carrying all their gear on their backs, and many who use a car or pickup, but pitch a tent for the night. I no longer hoof it, as I lack the energy of youth; or perhaps as a youth I lacked the money to pay for a vehicle and gas. Today I use a motorcycle, which carries more than twice what a backpacker can, but I still ride slowly through the mountains, and stop often just to look. There are just as many light-weight campers; indeed, there are more. But the majority today do not truly camp. They have trailers, big trailers, some as big as mobile homes. They have fifth-wheels, toy-haulers and motor homes. They have large bedrooms and bathrooms, showers, freezers, refrigerators, air conditioners, complete kitchens and roomy storage. They have mobile apartments. They have stereos and microwave ovens, televisions and satellite dishes. But they do not have a tent.

Such machines do get people to the Great Outdoors. After a day of fishing and boating, or seeing the sights, or hiking through the forests or canyons, they return to their "camp", fire up the generator, whose noise drowns the whisper of the wind in the trees and frightens off the wildlife, whose fumes mask the perfume of the forest. The lights come on, driving back the darkness. Instead of dimly seeing the whole world around them, they see a bright circle of a picnic table and a vehicle enclosed in a solid wall of black. The stars vanish from the sky. Then they open the door and step back into the city they thought they had left, move their packaged dinner from the freezer to the microwave, and turn on the satellite TV to watch their current sit-com or, ironically, a "reality" show. Then sleep till three hours after dawn.

If that is what they like, it is okay. They do experience the wild world, at least in part, with their accustomed comforts, and, most importantly, have fun. But they should be aware that they are missing more than half of the wild, of the beauty and the wonder. Perhaps, for some, it is the right choice.

Forty years ago, and more, it was simpler, though not easier. Still, I wonder what campers of forty years before that, or a hundred, would have thought of my early camping, or of my style and gear today. I have studied the first edition Boy Scout's Handbook, and the works of Nessmuk, Beard, Harding, Seton, Kreps, and others. They were woodsmen, trappers and explorers, "outers", of fifty and a hundred years before. They made most of their own gear, or could make it. They scorned sleeping bags, claiming blankets kept them warmer, and could be used for other purposes as well. They rarely carried tents, preferring a rectangle of cotton canvas. They built fires with bow drills or with flint and steel, but praised the new-fangled Lucifer matches, and used them till they ran out. They carried no prepared food, but rather a side of bacon and bags of beans, cornmeal and flour. Fresh meat they shot along the way. They sometimes had pack-beasts, horses or mules or dogs, or canoes. If not, they carried everything themselves. They repaired their gear in the field, eking years or decades of use from each item.

But they were no fools. There is much modern gear they would have adopted eagerly. Such as a disposable butane lighter, which will replace a thousand matches, and is much smaller and lighter. Or modern sleeping bags, far superior to blankets, and lighter. And hand-cranked flashlights would be ranked as indispensable! But not all modern gear would be adopted; their insect repellent was more effective than any modern one I have tried. Their knives and axes were better than most available today. Modern tents, though lighter and easier to pitch, do not last long, only two or three seasons, and are useless in severe weather. And most camping styles today they would not consider camping at all, surely no style that does not involve a tent, or sleeping in the open. Most modern camping gear would be of no value to them, even leaving out the "gear" that is not properly part of camping at all, such as satellite dishes and microwave ovens and the many useless gadgets and "comforts" too numerous and heavy to carry. Most of them are "nice to have", but not actually *needed*.

Camping conditions have changed as much as the camping gear. Indeed, much gear is useful only because conditions have changed. Many streams and lakes are no longer safe to drink from, and campers and hikers are warned not to drink from any of them unless they use a purifier. Actually, most mountain streams are quite clean, but for the ignorant and delicate city-folk, it is better take no chances. Nessmuk writes of setting up an overnight camp, starting with cutting down a dozen spruce saplings to use as bedding and shelter. That was acceptable when there were few campers. Today, entire forests would be denuded if most campers were so profligate about gathering material. Indeed, in most forests, it is illegal to cut even a single green branch. Nessmuk and his compadres did that daily just to make shelters and beds and even cooking skewers. With so many people in the woods, we must have restrictions, and we must tread lightly to preserve the wilds.

And the changes will continue. Camping next century may be unrecognizable. Today, most campgrounds will limit visitors to two weeks, then they must go elsewhere. Perhaps the limit will be two weeks per year, with reservations made at least six months in advance, then no more camping anywhere for the rest of the year. Perhaps there will be no dispersed camping at all, only stays in developed campgrounds. No gathering firewood. Cook only in a charcoal grill, or over a "campfire" of concrete "logs" burning piped-in natural gas. Swimming pools by the lakes, so we do not contaminate the waters. Paved hiking trails, and if you step off the pavement or litter the land, you will be banned from camping for the rest of your life. It is a dreary prospect, but the alternative is worse. Imagine a hundred million people camping as Nessmuk did. There would be no wilds at all.

It could happen. It could be worse. It certainly will be more restricted that it is today. Until, of course, civilization collapses and we enter a new Dark Age. Then we shall return to Nessmuk's methods. Might as well enjoy it while we can.

Weekend Round-Up

It had been a long day. Normally I only ride a hundred or a hundred-fifty miles from one camp to another, but today I had come over three hundred. Almost nine hours in the saddle, with about a dozen stops, two to get gas, three to wait for the road crew to let traffic through, the rest to just look. I was tired, and a bit sore when I reached the campground where I planned to spend the weekend, nine thousand feet up and fifty miles from Denver. It was Thursday, and the campground was, as expected, empty, no one there at all. But every site, every single one, had a pair of notices posted, reserving them for this weekend, and reserving them for the next. All of them - - - save one. Maybe they have a rule that one site must be left unreserved. Maybe I am just lucky.

I took the site, paid my fee, and settled in. It was peaceful, lonesome, quiet, a perfect place to experience aloneness. Nothing but the trees, and the clouds, and the occasional lowing of a not-distant-enough cow. Quite acceptable.

And now it is dawn. The sun is just appearing, and the temperature is thirty-eight degrees. Having just fled from hundred degree weather in Arizona and New Mexico, I bask in the welcome chill, and contemplate my good fortune to be here and live like this. My thoughts turn to my neighbors soon to arrive. It is five AM, six to them, because they like to label time differently. There is a harsh noise bellowing in their ears, forcing them awake. Grumbling, they perform ritualized morning ablutions, then have their first cup of coffee, and finally wake up. They eat, then the men tie nooses around their necks, and the women don their American burkhas (they call it "make-up") to conceal their faces. I have no idea what their children do, twenty-first century city kids on summer vacation. At any rate, off they all go to work (pardon my French), or whatever it is they do. But they will be less than efficient today, for while their bodies will be present, the better part of their minds will be - - - right here, where I am now. They will sit with bovine stares, their minds in Saturday and Sunday morning, hiking and loafing and "roughing it".

I expect a couple to arrive in the early afternoon, having taken an extra half-day off. Some will arrive in mid-afternoon, but most will stampede from their offices at five or five-thirty and not make it up here till an hour or two before dark. Dark is about nine o'clock their time. Some will be disappointed at finding there is a campfire ban in effect; they will have to sit around their propane stoves to toast their marshmallows. But they will be here, they will be out of the city and in the clean, cool air, gazing at the massed unnaturally crowded trees, raptly listening to the sounds of wildlife, the chittering of the cheery chipmunks, the bugling of the, ahem, cows. (To them, it is not people or pets, so it is wildlife!) They will have fun.

Yes, I make fun of the city-folk in the wilds. Often I am scornful. But I am not contemptuous of the *people* (most of them), but of their failure to *think*. They know how to camp, and hike, and fish. They saw it on TV. They have already learned how, so there is no need to learn any more. I have been camping for years, continuously, and am quite expert at it. And I learn something new every single day, about camping, about the Wilds, about people, about myself. One's mind must be open and flowing like a brook; the closed mind is stagnant, a puddle of mud and stinking mire in the midst of a pasture. My contempt is reserved for the mud-minded. My efforts are to open a flow. The smallest trickle will expand the puddle, will cause it to overflow, widen it to allow more and more flow. In time, the scummy puddle will become a pristine pool, but will only remain so while the flow is maintained. Stop the flow, close the channel, and the pond will stagnate again, and soon diminish and degrade, a mere puddle, to dry and become dust.

Let us see what kind of people come.

Eleven o'clock, I hear a motor approaching. The first arrival. No, it is only the trash collector.

Noon. A car! A pickup truck! No, it is a man from the hosting company, checking the campground to make sure it is ready. He tells me that I am in the camp host site, but just last week it had been decided to not keep resident hosts at this campground, and they had been moved elsewhere. As I said, lucky. We shoot the bull for a bit, then he leaves.

Finally, a camper. Alas, he is a maverick, for he has no reservation. I pull out a forest map and we note a few other campgrounds he can try. I suggest he go further from the city, and wish him luck. He will need it, and I can spare some.

The sky has clouded over, an almost unbroken overcast. A tiny patch of blue here, another to the other side. Gray, and growing darker. Shortly after two, the deluge begins. First a pickup pulling a fifth-wheel, then a sedan with the second-smallest trailer I have ever seen. A car with a pop-up, a pickup with a camper in the bed, six, eight, nine of them, but five must leave. Sorry, campground full. All in twenty minutes. These are the ones who knocked off at noon.

The first generator starts at two-thirty, but it is not enough to drown out the hooting of the cows, and does not last long.

An hour later, a late arrival. Perhaps they had some last-minute task. No, they have three small children, three, four and five years old. At home, they are no doubt rug-rats and house-apes; rounding them up and getting them ready (Did you go potty?) entailed an extra hour. The little ones leap from the car and race about, shouting in delight their wondrous world-shattering discoveries: A tree taller than their apartment-house! A rock bigger than the car! A chipmunk! Is that Alvin? Oh, listen to the cows barking! They scamper about as Daddy sets up the tent, their high-piping voices overlapping, blending, their words just barely unintelligible, for they are now speaking the language of the streams, a babbling brood rinsing the air with happy music. Campgrounds *need* children.

A steady stream of would-be campers passes through, around and around, wistfully seeking a spot that does not exist, not here, not now. They bawl in despair "Isn't there a single site not taken?" The cows answer "Noooo".

At long last, the main body of the herd arrives. The first ones, the ones who planned ahead, who packed in advance, fought their way home through the nightly trail drive, loaded their last-minute store of perishable chuck, and headed for the hills. They find the sites marked with their brands and they unharness their rigs. For two hours more they straggle in, accompanied by many mavericks and strays now desperately questing for an open site. Soon it will be dark,and they will run out of time. Some will settle for a dispersed camp, some will succumb and stay in a motel. Some may give up and go back to Denver, their weekend spoilt. There they will console themselves with a case of beer and "reality" TV. As darkness falls and the cows trudge off to roost for the night, the last laggard arrives and slips into his stall. He raises his pop-up and levels it by moonlight as his wife prepares a meal. I have already eaten my rough outdoor fare of spaghetti in marinara sauce, so now I retire to my tent, accompanied by the remote wail of a lonely bull baying at the moon.

I awake at first cow-crow and emerge to a glorious mountain morning. The sky is clear, only a few tiny wisps of high cirrus counterpointing the blue. Heavy dew glistens on every flat surface, and the air is still and cool. No fires are allowed, so I must eschew my morning warmer. Instead, I walk in the meadows and open thickets till the sun arises, then return to sit in the warm glow. The air drifts gently as the dew sparkles and evaporates. The dogies are enjoying a morning stroll, pulling along their well-trained owners whom they have brought along to pick up their messes. Two young women, late teens, wear heavy parkas and short-shorts, their legs bare. Small children run by, racing and laughing to the out-houses. One good thing about Daylight Saving Time: City campers, who must live by the clock even out here, are more likely to experience the early morning, or at least an hour more of it. Surprisingly, almost everyone seems to be up and about, and it is only half an hour after sunrise. These are people, good people, and they are rewarded for their lack of sloth: Aspens flicker in the breeze, chipmunks scamper in the grass, cows sing in the field. And no generators. The first arrival ran one as soon as he got here, but for less than an hour. Since then, I have not heard a one. No motor homes, either. Only one fifth-wheel. Several sites with tents. They all seem to know what they are doing. It is very refreshing, rare and satisfying. Even the one latecomer was late, not from poor planning, but from a flat tire.

I stroll through the campground, meeting old friends for the first time.

End of a Season

The seasons come, the seasons go, and once again, we cross the Great Divide. Or, I should say, *another* Great Divide, for there are several. I refer, here to the Camping Divide, the annual demarcation between casual campers and road residents. The Hunters and Winter Sporters are different groups, though many of them do camp. The casual campers are those who ride their RV (frequently rented) to some developed campground to Rough It and See the Sights for a weekend or a week.

Beginning Memorial Day Weekend, the Camping Season starts. Campgrounds in the high montane open, and Winter-weary city-folk flock to the recently empty forests and parks, filling them to capacity (at least on weekends). For the next three months, experienced road residents strive to *never* arrive at a campground on Friday or Saturday, unless they have a reservation. You might find a spot, but the odds are very much against you. It can be rather amusing to watch the endless cavalcade of optimists and the ignorant parading through a campground on a holiday weekend, usually on a Saturday, desperately seeking an unoccupied sanctuary. It happens every weekend, but especially on the long weekends, at almost every campground I have been in. It is even funnier to see one actually find a free spot. They are usually quite smug about it, and often brag about how they *always* find a spot. *Sure* they do. And how many days does it take them?

This state of affairs continues right through the Labor Day Weekend, which is generally the most intense and heavily crowded time. The casual campers are getting in their last licks, their last chance to go camping before the kids go back to school. They tend to get up earlier and go to bed later than they do on other holidays. They also depart on Monday somewhat later than usual. Cramming in every minute of freedom that they possibly can, for they shall be bound to their tasks, chained to their desks, for the next nine months, till Memorial Day rolls around again, and a new season begins.

And here it is, Labor Day Weekend. I arrived early on Wednesday, and had my choice, any one of the sixteen empty sites out of twenty in the campground. Naturally, I took the best one. I had arrived about eleven; by dusk, there were ten left. Thursday saw six more occupied, and the last four were taken by noon on Friday. And then the parade began. Motor homes, fifth-wheels, toy haulers, trailers of all sizes, pickup campers and even a couple of trailerless cars wandered through, some of them making a second circuit in their desperation, but all, alas, doomed to bitter disappointment, forced to seek another site. Perhaps they settled for dispersed camping. Perhaps they sought shelter in in some commercial campground or lodge, or submitted to a motel, if they could find one. They must sleep *somewhere!* One site across from mine was abandoned about dusk, which is quite odd, almost unheard of. The parade had ended, and, unlikely though it is, no late-night straggler wandered through, But the next morning, between dawn and sunrise, the first seeker appeared and glommed on to the site. Oh, was he smug! Oh, was he ever pleased with himself! "See!", he told his wife. "Arrive early! Never fails!" Poor bloke has no idea how lucky he was.

It is not uncommon to have people leave, even on the holiday weekends, on Saturday or Sunday. Some have a long drive to get home on time. Some have made a series of one-day reservations, and are cramming as many events as they can into their last vacation. When they do, the next parader gets his lucky break. It is rare for an opened site to last as much as twenty minutes; I have, not rarely, seen the newcomer take possession before the previous occupant was out of sight. In a way, this is unfortunate, for it gives the mavericks hope, it encourages them to continue their random and unplanned ways. On the other hand, it is a game; there is always a chance to win. And people will risk much on small chances. Just look at how much profit the gambling casinos rake in. For Indians, casinos are a more profitable scam even than dream-catchers!

This campground is high in the mountains of Wyoming, high enough that even in late August, the temperature drops below freezing almost every night. This helps to discourage the inexperienced, and provides me with preferable neighbors. But it is also near to Yellowstone and Grand Teton National Parks. They, I guarantee you, are packed full, every campsite for every night of the Labor Day Weekend, and for several days on either side. The dozens of campgrounds clustering around their borders are likewise full, for these National Parks are to tourists what lamps are to moths, and none are brighter than Yellowstone. But this one is a bit farther, and off the main routes, and it does not allow reservations. They have become quite rare in the National Forests, these campgrounds that are one hundred percent first-come-first-served. Some of the overflow reaches this far. Not much, but some. Most of my neighbors are kindred souls, many of them characters. One is a painter, the most skilled and talented I have ever met. Another is an amateur astronomer, here because this area is one of the darkest in the country, one of the best for star-gazing. He came to the area by intent, and then stumbled upon this campground, probably the best for star-gazing, by accident. He came for one night. Nine days ago.

But there is another, a recently retired couple, on their second or third trip. They are knowledgable, but at the same time inexperienced; they have much book-learning, but little practical application. Very much like I was when I first set out in the seventies. Today they made a big, big mistake. I was walking by their site, and their pickup was gone; they were off on some day-trip. A column of smoke rose from their firepit. On investigation, the pit turned out to hold only white ashes, and one foot-long chunk of eight-inch log. Clearly, their fire had been, to the eye, dead and out. But a tiny coal in a log can persist for days, even a week or more, then grow and flame and scatter sparks in the wind. Their late fire was far from dead, decidedly unsafe. I got a bucket of water, soaked the log, and drenched the pit. The true irony of this lies in their lack of experience. They know better. They do! Just this morning, we were talking about wildfires. They mentioned one in North Carolina, where a troop of Boy Scouts had left their fire scattered and buried, but not drenched, and it had revived and scorched a large part of the Great Smoky Mountains. Exactly the situation they had potentially created here. I shall chastise them, but if they do it again, I will call a Ranger, and watch over the fire till he arrives.

I respect the Forest Service, greatly. They are at least trying. But they can, on occasion, *be* trying. The Rangers and Volunteers and Fire Fighters and Station Staff are almost invariably fine, intelligent, pleasant people, good at their jobs, and dedicated. They do this work because they love the Wilds. However, they are bossed by the bureaucrats, who are, well, bureaucrats. I expect they are mostly Easterners who think their local conditions apply nationally, and thus make poor decisions. Like ordering a Prescribed Burn when conditions are calm, though Fire Danger is extreme, ignoring the forecast for high winds in three days. "Oh, there is no danger. The burn will be finished before that."

It was named the Diener Canyon Fire of 2018.

Today the Season is over. This campground will close for the Winter next week. The dirt road is in pretty good shape, no ruts, only a few small potholes. The winter rains and snows will likely tear it up some, requiring grading next Spring to open it up for next crop of clients. But almost no one will use it till then. So why did they send a grader to smooth the road today? Did anybody actually *think* about this?

The campground has emptied. By Monday night, only four sites were still occupied. At one of those, the camper left, but the site was reoccupied not ten minutes later. Still, the weekend is over. The season is over. The campground will be barely used for the next week or so, then closed down.

Oh, yeah? Tuesday morning an overnighter leaves. Then a new one pulls in, and another, and another. Three trailers arrive at once. The first one grabs the site across the road from me. The second takes the next open one off to my left. The third finds one out of sight behind me. I am treated to an impromptu Concerto for Three Campers in SurroundSound: "Left a little." "Okay, pull it back!" "Turn it the other way!" "Hold it!" "That's enough!" "Stop!" They all three finish up in just a couple of minutes. Fastest I have seen in a long time. These folks know what they are doing, and probably are gold friends. My plan to depart tomorrow leaves little time to get to know them. Or the four I see pulling in now. One, two, three sites remain, and it is only four o'clock.

I believe I shall stay one more day.

Changing of the Guard

September, at eight thousand feet, in the cool mountains of northeastern Utah. Most of the people are gone, the summer Tourists with their portable apartments packed with comforts and luxuries, with children and the toys to keep them amused while vacationing in "the country", all gone, back to cities and jobs and schools. I do not begrudge them the use of the forests, for the land is as much theirs as it is mine, and it is good that children learn a taste for it, learn to understand it and respect it. But few of them do truly appreciate it, and in some ways I am glad they are gone.

The Hunters have begun to arrive, armed with bows, then black powder, then modern rifles. These are generally a better class of people, for where the tourist sees the forest and the wildlife, the hunter sees aspen and birch, pine and fir, oak and elm, and recognizes the animals and birds. He knows their habits and needs. He appreciates it more deeply. I laugh at the city conservationists and tree-huggers who treasure a concept, an idea of Unspoiled Nature, and denounce the hunters who "despoil" nature. Ha! The hunters have a far greater love for and understanding of Nature, and most of them work actively to conserve and protect it.

The Vagabonds are more prominent, now. Always the same numbers, but a much higher proportion, now that the summer population is gone. These are mostly retired folk or independently wealthy; much the same thing, really. Yes, almost all are rich. If their pension is nine hundred dollars a month, and they only need eight hundred, is that not wealth and independence? Plus their real estate, tens of thousands of square miles of prime forest and field. And time; they have all of the time in the world! These are the people who know and love the wild. They are a part of the eco-system, and they know it. It is a different population now, smaller and quieter, and the difference is obvious.

And the Wild is changing, too. The conifers are still ever green, but the deciduous trees feel the cooling season. Some are still green, but the color is pale and wan. Yellow abounds, and orange and red are common. Climb the long road from the plain to the pass. As the altitude rises, the spectrum drops, the blue and green giving way to yellow, orange, red. At eleven thousand feet, the trees at the pass are all evergreens, but just below, leaves are beginning to fall. Soon there will be bare boughs, and it will take more than a glance to tell the dead snags from the sleeping living. Then the guard will change again, from ATVs and hikers to snowmobiles and skiers. The vegetation will sleep beneath the snow, along with most of the animals. The birds will mostly be far to the south, along with most of the Vagabonds.

I will not see it, for I am a Vagabond, and I, too, will be far south. Winter is the time for the deep desert, for the plains and lowlands of New Mexico and Arizona and southern Texas, where winter is the season of dry, not of snow.

Four-Legs

Ow Ow Ow Owwww!

A choice that has always faced people is that between liberty and security. As a general rule, most choose security. "Safety First", and all of that. I will not argue here which is the better choice, only state that I choose Liberty.

The Canids made that choice, many millenia ago. Man came among them, and they watched him, and soon came to understand, more or less, what he did, and what he might be capable of. Some of them decided it would be a good idea to team up with the Two-Legs, and did so, and became *Canis domesticus*, the domesticated dog. They chose security, and lost virtually all of their liberty. Others felt the price was too high, and chose to remain free. They became *Canis latrans*, the "barking dog", the prairie wolf, the coyote.

There is no doubt that the coyote is smarter than the dog. Much smarter. Sure, a dog can learn tricks like roll over and sit and stay. But take one look at a tied dog who has wrapped his rope around a tree and cannot for the life of him figure out how to unwrap it, and try to claim that dog is smart. I have known exactly one dog who was smart enough to disentangle himself. (He even knew how to trick other dogs into getting all snarled up, then sit just out of reach and laugh at them.) Coyotes, on the other hand, have figured out guns and poisons and roads. They can tell the difference between a stick and a rifle. When I am carrying a stick, I often see coyotes; when I am carrying a rifle, they are rare, and if I do see one, he is generally vanishing in the brush. Ranchers set out poisoned baits to kill wolves who prey on their calves and lambs. Such baits can be quite effective on wolves, but not on coyotes. The coyotes will scavenge. If they find the carcass of a deer or an elk, they will gladly eat it. They will pick up a quick bit of take-out from the road. But a piece of meat left out by a two-leg? They pass it by. Usually. I knew a man in Los Angeles, who lived in his car, and often bought cans of dog food to feed the coyotes. They never hesitated to eat it. One night he gave me a can, and I set it out for his friends. A coyote found it, sniffed, and backed away. He looked around and spotted my friend, and only then did he eat the food. I have also known them to take food from campgrounds, but never around farms or ranches. Not food that has been left out for them. This is not instinct, it is reasoned behavior. They will steal picnic lunches, given the chance, and truck from gardens. Did you know, in the Southwest, coyotes eat chile peppers? True, They chew up the fruit and spit out the seeds. I have also seen a lot of roadkill, usually squirrels and rabbits, sometimes deer, skunks, and even raccoons. But I have never seen a run-over turkey, and only once a coyote. A very young coyote. I *have* seen struck dogs, many of them. One of my own, the smartest dog I ever owned, was killed by a car.

Dogs also have a very limited vocabulary. They can learn to understand many human words, but have few of their own. Coyotes have a large and intricate language. They have long and varied gab-fests, choruses of yips, barks and howls, clear exchanges of information. If you are persistent and fortunate, you can sometimes observe them while they are calling, and see what they do. Sometimes a lone coyote will howl, receive an answer, howl again, then shut up and sit and wait. Soon his companions come to him. Other times, instead of sitting he will trot off to join the others. Clearly, the pack had come to an agreement as to who should go to whom. Once I watched five coyotes confer, then four of them went off to either side and vanished, leaving one, a bitch, standing in the open. About two minutes later, a wandering dog approached. The lone coyote yipped, took a couple of steps towards him, then a couple away. The dog gave a soft bark and trotted up to her, at which point the other four leaped from hiding and killed the dog. They had planned and executed a sophisticated ambush, and gained an easy meal.

Dogs are very flighty and easily distracted, and do not seem capable of holding on to an idea for very long. Watch a dog wandering the outdoors. He will zig-zag all over, stopping to sniff a bush or a tree here and there, chasing a squirrel or a rabbit or a butterfly. He may tree a squirrel, then forget it and wander off to something else that catches his interest. Coyotes do not behave like that. I have never seen one wander, zig-zag, or even stroll. Always they trot along in a straight line, going somewhere with a clear destination in mind. They will change course to avoid a two-leg or to catch an opportune meal, but other than that, show a steady and unswerving determination.

One might think the coyotes are too independent to form an inter-species partnership, but that is not the case. They will do so, if they can be the boss, or at least not an underling. Their usual tactic for digging out rodents (their staple food) is for one coyote to dig at a den while a second stands guard near the alternate entrance (rodents always have at least two tunnels to their hole). When the rodent attempts to escape, the watcher snaps it up, and splits it with the digger. Sometimes (and it is not at all uncommon), a coyote will team up with a badger to do the same job. The badger, much better at digging, chases the rodent out, and the coyote, faster and smarter, catches the meal, which they share. Then the coyote herds the badger to another hole, and they do it again.

Coyotes will kill other coyotes, but apparantly prefer not to. When I lived in Los Angeles, I often saw coyotes running around residential sections at night. Many times, the animals were hobbling on three legs. Once I saw a pack of four, each with a crippled leg. It puzzled me for a while. What could be breaking their legs? Traps could do it, but their were no traps. One night I saw the answer. A lone coyote was set upon by a small pack. Apparantly the loner was encroaching on the pack's territory. They surrounded him and knocked him to the ground, whereupon the largest coyote grabbed one leg in his mouth, and broke it. I could clearly hear the snap. They then left the helpless one, who limped away as fast as he could. They could have killed and eaten him, but they let him off with a warning. A very severe warning, but they let him live.

I am a friend to coyotes. I will not injure them, nor hunt them gratuitously. I respect them, and admire them. Not that they care. They see no advantage in such a friendship. They will tolerate me, and depart if I should approach. Sure, I could be a source of food, and protection. I could make their lives easier, for a few of them. But they do not *need* anything from me. They are quite capable of finding enough food on their own, and defending themselves from most hazards. They have enough security, and if they occasionally run into something that is more than they can handle, well, that is how life is. There is no perfect safety; there cannot be, and they know it full well. So they keep their freedom, their independence.

Live free, or die.

Squirrels

Squirrels are such a lovely nuisance! Their comical antics can always paint a smile on my face, and often provide a laugh as well, and that is all the more amusing, as they seem to believe that every laugh is at them. They are remarkably sensitive and insecure critters, as easily insulted as cats. They can always be embarrassed and made to feel foolish. A tree squirrel was once scrounging my camp for scraps when a chipmunk not even a quarter of his size poked up his head. The startled squirrel invoked survival panic, fled to a nearby pine, and levitated ten feet to a branch. I laughed and said "Scared by a chipmunk, huh?" The squirrel scolded as mightily as I have ever heard.

I know of no more active animal, unless you count the chipmunk as separate. They are constantly popping up in the most unexpected places. Even in my essays, when I have no thought of the pestiferous insects, one of the gate-crashing hams will insert himself for a stolen cameo. If I am writing of the morning light highlighting the needles of a fir, a squirrel will interject himself, silhouetted against the sky, a black form with his fur-tips all ablaze. Or when I am deep in describing the soft comfort of the pre-dawn mists and the splendid silence of the not yet awakened world, suddenly the quiet is perforated by the piercing barks of a squirrel. They intrude their chatter into a songbirds' chorus, or get into an argument with a camp-robber jay. Always they will appear, sometimes supplying a welcome grace note, other times shattering a mood as a pebble fragments reflections in a mirror-smooth pool. They are a part of Nature and, like it or not, they *will* be present.

One may get the impression from my tales that I dislike squirrels. They are quite a nuisance, often obnoxious, and I frequently insult and disrespect them. I enjoy playing pranks on them (you may have read "A Tiny Tale of Terror"), but it is all a game, for they play pranks on me, and on others as well. For example, I once left a half-dozen cookies on the table while I sat and made some notes. After a few minutes, I noticed a squirrel sitting up ten feet away, looking at me, with a cookie in his mouth. As soon as I saw him, he scampered off. When I checked the table, there were only three cookies. He was stealing them, four feet from me, and making sure that I knew he was the culprit. But I do like them. Especially fried in bacon grease. They are a necessary part of Nature, and enrich not only the forest, but also our experience of the Wild. They are superb mirrors for our imaginations, reflecting our ideas of their ideas, of their motivations and desires. For squirrels have all of these, though the truth is far different from what we ascribe to them.

All campers have seen squirrels beg. They sit up on their hind legs, tuck their forepaws above their chubby protruding tummies, and stare with big plaintive Bambi eyes. "Oh, please," they seem to say, "Please toss a crust to a poor starving harmless orphan! A fox ate my father and a hawk took my mother, and I am so pitiful and alone!" It is a lie. Like a "homeless" panhandler who rakes in two or three hundred dollars a day, the squirrel is playing on your sympathy. Look at his big bulging belly. He is fat! He gorges his greedy gut on goodies extorted from gullible humans. The squirrels have campers well trained to throw food at sitting squirrels. If you do not throw food, and even if you do, as soon as your back is turned, they will swarm up onto your picnic table and steal anything that smells tasty. Yogi Bear is a piker in comparison.

Squirrels are little more than food-gathering machines. They will gather whatever they can find and eat till their bellies are full, then continue to gather just as energetically, stashing the food in hollow trees and rock crevices, burying nuts in shallow holes. "Oh, look, mommy, the squirrel is planting a tree!" Sorry, honey, he will also "plant" a bread crust. Each squirrel has dozens of caches, any one of which would feed him through half the winter. He needs so many because he forgets where they are, and probably only re-discovers them by accident, or finds a stash left by some other squirrel. They do not do this because they are smart or clever. Ravens are smart. Coyotes are clever. Squirrels are - - - well, stupid! A squirrel found a woodpeckers' larder tree, where the birds bored deep holes, then stuffed acorns in for winter fodder. The squirrel would extract an acorn and carry it to another tree where he placed it in a hollow, then dash back for another, and another, and another. But a young woodpecker had found the hollow, and just as industriously was stealing nuts and inserting them back in the same tree the squirrel was robbing. I watched them for almost a full hour; it was the best laugh I had enjoyed in months, better even than a Roadrunner cartoon. Eventually, an older woodpecker arrived and assessed the situation. He summoned the clans, and a dozen woodpeckers assembled and harrassed and worried the squirrel till he fled to a fortress of thick branches. From this refuge, he chattered dire threats and dreadful curses as the flock emptied his hollow and returned their pilfered property to the larder tree. Do you see? You can attribute human emotions and values to a pitiful and begging scavenger, and I can do the same with a flock of red-headed bird-brains.

Never trust a squirrel. They understand food and fear, and nothing else. Throw rocks at them, and they will dodge, or ignore you. Chase them and they will come back at once. Terrify them - - - Ah, *that* they will remember. I was sitting in my chair, unmoving, watching the world, smelling the spruce, delighting in the birdsong, when a plump Archer's squirrel bounded up. He was an odd one, for his belly and tail were both dark; usually one or the other is white. He looked me over, suspecting I might be a human, but deducing I was not, because I did not move. He dismissed me and looked over the camp. He hopped onto the table, but there was nothing edible lying around (not in *my* camp). He spotted my tent, eighteen, twenty feet away. He must have known about tents, had probably robbed them before, so he ran and leaped over the foot-high sill. I seized the opportunity, and my staff, and light-footed over. I stepped inside and swept the door-flap closed behind me. The squirrel, frozen in shock, stared at me, his eyes twice the size of his head. I stared back, striving to appear as horrible and hungry as I could. I smiled, and opened my mouth; the squirrel darted away and cowered in a corner. My staff extended toward him and he dashed to the other corner. Again the staff moved; he leaped and bounced off the fabric. He could not climb, could not burrow, could not hide, could only panic. I chased him relentlessly, once faking a thrust then stabbing the staff into his path. He turned in mid-leap and actually skidded backwards, scrabbling for traction and striking the staff before he wore out his momentum. Twenty, thirty, forty times I herded the rabid rodent forth and back. When it seemed he could hardly stand, I stepped aside and drew back the door fly. I pointed at little Albert and said "Leave!" For the only time ever, a squirrel obeyed me. He shot from the tent and vanished in the brush, thoroughly chased and chastened. Though I stayed there another week, I never, *never,* saw that squirrel again. I could have left out a cornucopia of every tasty treat he could dream of, and he would not have returned. I expect I also saved some future city-camper from the anguish of finding her fresh loaf of bread with a squirrel-hole tunneled through the center. You may say I behaved meanly and cruelly. If so, you do not understand Nature, nor squirrels. You would not call the grizzly who chased *me* up a tree mean or cruel.

Cute little squirrels can be quite amoral, and vicious. I have seen them fight each other, for mates, for territory. I have seen one tear out the throat of another, then continue biting as his victim bled to death. I have seen one rip open the belly of an opponent, then pursue as the disembowelled one attempted to flee, trampling his own intestines. Cute, harmless, innocent creatures. Part of Nature, "red of tooth and claw". Many, many more times I have seen them at play, one chasing another till he caught him and tumbled him in the dust, then fleeing as the tumbled one chased him in turn, over and over, playing a frolicsome game of tag, interrupted only by an occasional break to stand erect, scanning for assurance of no impending danger. I have watched a pair of chipmunks standing, licking and patting each other's faces, teenagers petting and spooning, necking and canoodling. I have seen a mother courageously scolding and defying me as her young dove for cover, before scampering for shelter herself.

The common conception, the Disney model, is so inadequate, so one-dimensional. These animals are living beings, as complex, in their own ways, as humans. Wolves are not just vicious, single-minded killers. Deer are not simply kind and loving Bambis. They are those things, but many more besides. Like the six blind men, you will never understand the elephant if you hold to one narrow view. Nature is simple, and at the same time, complex. All that are part of her, bird and beast, rock and tree, river and human, all are also simple and complex, and part of the whole. Do not deride the hunter for killing the deer, for it is part of the deer's nature and purpose to be hunted. Do not condemn the cougar for hunting deer, for that is its nature. Do not scoff at the rabbit for being timid, for that is how it survives. And do not coo over the cute little lovey-dovey squirrel for being such a cute little lovey-dovey, nor despise it for being a sneak thief and a callous spoiler of picnic lunches. See and accept the squirrel for what he is, and take proper precautions against his depredations. They can easily ruin your vacation if you are careless or ignorant.

But the forest would be a sadder place if they should all cease to be.

A Tiny Tale of Terror

Poor little chipper. Some people call him a striped ground squirrel, but I call him a chipmunk, because that is what he is. I was sitting in my chair, five feet from a lonesome fir, just listening, watching, not moving, being part of the forest. The stupid little chipmunk couldn't figure me out. Apparantly decided I was not a human, because I did not move or make cutesy noises at him. So he came over and hopped up on my cuff. I looked at him and said, quietly, "Boo!" Bang! Off he went and scuttled up the tree so fast that he set a new all-forest record! He stared at me, panting, stunned, wholly unbelieving of this new human perfidy, appalled at the lengths we would go to harass a helpless, harmless creature. Then he set in to scolding, taking me to task for tormenting a poor inoffensive orphan. So I scolded him back. "Stupid-stupid-stupid-stupid-stupid. Cowardly chicken-munk! Tree-rat!" I ladled on the insults, laughing all the while, dissecting his character and lack of moral fortitude. As soon as I stopped, he would chatter and scold some more. As soon as he stopped, I would resume. I told him I was calling him more than three names, but he couldn't tell because his tiny incompetent mind couldn't remember more. As soon as I voiced the fourth, he forgot the first. He chattered back indignantly, as only a squirrel can. We traded insults for at least ten minutes. If you are at all familiar with these foolish fluffheads, you know they almost never scold for more than a minute at a time; they are incapable of holding an idea any longer. Their train of thought is no more than a locomotive and a caboose. The really smart ones may add a coal-car. I asked if he wasn't hungry. He called me a chitter. I told him he could just stay there, because I was not moving. He missed the joke, and called me a chitter. I told him it was a pity he could not jump the fifteen feet to the next tree. He tried to think about that, and failed, and called me a chitter. I told him "Fine, stay there. You could get down and away easily enough. I don't move that fast. But you are too stupid." He chattered back "Stoo-pit! Stoo-pit! Stoo-pit!"

I ignored him and went back to being the forest. After about fifteen minutes I heard a scratching sound. I looked, and the chipmunk had snuck half-way down the trunk. I did not say anything, I moved nothing more than my head, but the cowardly rodent dashed back up as fast as he could go, turned and scolded me anew. I pointed out that he had not one but two yellow streaks down his back. He gasped and called me a chitter. I told him he could come down now. Just stay on the other side of the tree. After all, if you can't see me, I can't see you. Right. He paused to think that one over, but in remembering how to pause, forgot to think.

The sun was moving, the shade shifting away, so I moved some twenty feet to another shadow. I told the chipmunk I would let him come down now. I sat and started writing this. I already know how it will end. Ten minutes or so, and the timorous twit is starting to come down. Twenty feet to go, fifteen, ten. I look straight at him and he is off like a shot - - - back up the tree, and scolding. Again. Calling me a chitter. I try to explain to him. "You think I am chitting? You think sitting still is not fair? You think it is chitting? You are so full of chit, it's all you can say! Listen! It is safe to come down! I won't chase you!" "Chitter! Chitter-chitter!"

It is another ten minutes before he tries again. This time I wait till he is only two feet off the ground before I look. He freezes. He stares. He tries to make up what little excuse he has for a mind, "Go back up? Leap to the ground and scamper away? This two-leg is tricky, he chits. Maybe he can magically move, suddenly appear in front of me and (eek!) *catch* me! He already said he would like to (shudder) eat me! Oh dear! Oh dear! Whatever do I do?" I doubt he ever resolved the quandary. I suppose the bark broke or his feet slipped, but somehow he dropped to the ground and dashed for the nearest tree, but it was a tree, and he had just been trapped in a tree, so he ran to another, but it was also a tree, and thus dangerous, so off he went to a third one. Maybe enough time had now passed for him to forget the idea that trees were traps, for he skittered up to safety. But this time he did not scold.

It was terrible fun, twitting that twit. And perhaps I was being a bully, engaging in a battle of wits against an unarmed opponent. I am sure that the chipmunk learned a lesson about messing with people. I am also sure he has completely forgotten it; after all, it was ten minutes ago. But the little thing has entertained me in recompense for ripped bread-wrappers and stolen food. A small amusement from a small creature.

It's the little things in life.

The Vixen

I was told there is a fox in this vicinity, with a clutch of kits.
This evening, she came to visit.   She was not the plump, fuzzy,
dark red object of
British fox hunts,
but fairly large,
well over a foot
at the shoulder,
and more a light
orange than red,
and lean, skinny,
as bad as a super-
model. She was,
as noted, quite
accustomed to
humans, passing
fearlessly within

fifteen feet of me, with only a glance or two askew. She knew
humans, was quite familiar with them and their inexplicable
trappings, known from experience to be no hazard to her, and
usually tending to leave quantities of food scattered about,
readily accessible.

Then she froze, dead still. She had sighted my motorcycle.
Apparantly she had never seen such a thing before. Bright red,
only two round feet, leaning aside, but not moving or toppling.
It smelled like the big noisy animals people ride in, but it was
too small. And lots of it was shiny and sparkly. She took a
couple of tentative steps, and it did nothing. She circled half

around, and it did nothing. She took one cautious step, then another, and another, and it did nothing. A camper snapped a branch at a nearby campsite, and the vixen leapt back five feet at a single bound, but the bike, it did nothing. Perhaps it was harmless, perhaps it was safe. Still unsure, she took a hesitant step forward, and after a pause, a second. As she approached, slowly, cautiously, a sudden breeze stirred the flag atop the bike. She vanished, dashing into the distance, diving into the brush. The bike still did nothing, but she has not returned. Perhaps she will investigate again in the morning, or next evening. Eventually, she will figure it out.

Well, she did. In the morning, I was enjoying a breakfast of fried eggs and fresh bannock when the vixen returned. She

stood between the bike and me, flirted her tail coquettishly and posed. I picked up my camera and managed to get one decent shot. She trotted a few feet up the hill, and paused. When I followed and again raised the camera, she stepped aside, interposing the tent between us. I followed again, stepping wide, but ... she was gone! Up the hill, off to the side, into the bush ... I could not tell. She was simply gone. I turned back to the fire and my interrupted meal, and there she was, making off with half of my bannock.

I had been out-foxed.

Beaver Dam

Most people think of a beaver dam as no more than a pile of branches that block the flow of water. They have never seen one, or if they have, they did not *look* at it. It starts with a foundation of just a tree dropped across the stream, then logs, as big as the beaver can move, and that can be pretty big. Smaller logs are interlaced with them, upstream where the water presses them against the foundation. Smaller and smaller branches are woven in till leaves and twigs will fill in the gaps and stop the water. Then it gets plastered with mud and made thicker and thicker. It is a solid and well-designed structure. Once the dam is in place, the water rises to form a pond. Often it will start to flow around the ends of the dam. When it does, the beaver builds wings, levees to extend the dam. In Shoshone National Forest in Wyoming I saw one where the beaver had built over fifty feet of dike, never as much as two feet tall. Mostly it was just mud a foot or so high, and maybe two feet thick. The taller parts had sticks embedded in the mud. The only water that got through was seepage under the levees and trickles through the main dam.

The beaver is building himself a home. Sometimes in the dam itself, more often in a sort of beaver-made island of mud and branches in the middle of the pond, there is a dry den, a room above water level, with several tunnels leading down and emerging underwater in the pond. The pond is as big as the beaver can make it, and, as in the one with low dikes, it is surrounded by shallow marsh, soggy ground well-planned to bog down most big predators. It is a fortress, a moated castle.

A predator has to struggle through the mire, then swim the pond, then somehow dig through a close grid of interlocking branches to reach the den. A grizzly *might* accomplish it, if he could get through the swamp. No wolf could.

The pond is also a larder. The beaver eats the inner bark of trees. During summer and fall, he fells trees, cuts off the branches, and hauls them into his pond, where he submerges them and locks them down, *under* the water. In winter, the food is below the frozen surface, where the beaver can get at it without exposing himself to predators. The grizzly is asleep, and the wolf can't break the ice.

A beaver taught me to cut firewood. If you look at the stump of a beaver-felled tree, you will see it has a conical shape, a blunt cone rising toward the center. The beaver gnaws it around and around till the trunk snaps off and the tree falls. Everyone who has cut firewood with a hatchet knows that the first chop or two cut deeper than the following chops. I cut as the beaver does, a couple of chops, turn the wood, a couple more, working all of the way around.   Sometimes the log cracks about that time. If not, I pick it up and slam it against the ground or over a rock, and it breaks. Either way, I do the job with a third of the effort in a third of the time it would take to just chop, chop, chop till at last the log is chopped through. Beavers know this.

People dismiss all of this as "instinct". The beavers "just know", genetically, how to pick the spot for a dam, how to build it so it stays there for a decade, how to build dikes and levees, how to build an unapproachable den, how to fell a tree with the least work, how and where to store winter food. It is simple to test: Raise a few generations of beaver in an old-style zoo, concrete floor, pool for swimming, no trees or branches except for food (unless you feed them Purina Beaver Chow). Release the fourth or fifth generation into the wild, at a suitable spot for a dam, and see what they do. If it is instinct, they will do as well as wild beaver. I strongly doubt that they would succeed. This is learned behavior, taught by the parents, passed down over the many millenia by the most successful ancestors, the ones who built the best dams and ponds. If it was all instinct, no beaver would get caught under a tree as it fell. It is rare, but it does happen.

Animals are not stupid. They observe, they learn, they teach their children. If you are quiet and unthreatening, you can watch them doing it. Watch a dog teaching her pups to hunt, or a cat teaching her kittens. Watch a squirrel teaching her young how to watch for hawks and foxes. Fresh-from-the-nest squirrellings tend to freeze in confusion at the new and unknown. Mamma teaches them to run, not freeze. These critters think, consciously. They learn. They figure things out. Just watch them, that is all.

You'll see.

The Pond

It is only a small pond, twenty to forty feet across. It lies in what was once a meadow, a very flat area, almost level, so flat that one must walk a hundred yards to find a place where water flows, five or six streamlets trickling through the grass. Farther upstream, not too far, one can find the single stream which is fragmented on the flat, carving a set of islands like some broad stepping-stones from one bank to the other.

The pond is no doubt shaped like a handprint in the mud, the broad palm visible before me, the fingers, hidden in the brush, extending ripple-less pools to the feeder streams emerging from amongst the islands. Or the pond may take the form of an irregular oval a hundred feet broad and three times as long. I know the fingers are there, for I have waded through the brush to see them. This is no poetic word-play; I *waded* through the brush, in water up to a foot deep, and mud even deeper, with brush and grass thick enough to hide the water, from view. Cresses and grasses and willow and cottonwood fill the fringes, which are the larger part of the pool itself, and flow into the dry land. But here between the soggy soil and the open water, no one can draw a line or set a post and say "Here the pond begins". If you climb the hill and look down upon the glen, you can clearly see

a body of deeper green surrounding the pond, but when you descend to the border between brown and green, you find that some brown sprouts from water, and some green grows in dust; the lush land does not correspond to the pond's marshy margin. And herein lies the secret of the pond: It is not a mere pond, not a chance formation, it is artificial, it was made. There is evidence, the litter of construction lying all around, if you look for it. Fallen trees, stumps with conical cuts, piles of chips three, four, five inches long, tracks and gullies in the grass, trails and traces of where heavy burdens were dragged to the water. Follow the trails, poke among the brush, and find the barrier that stops the stream's flow. Trunks and branches and twigs and mud, a thick dam, built by the beaver.

Now, the dam of a beaver is no random thing. He does not toss branches in the brook and hope that they will hang up somewhere. The site is clearly chosen with care, a narrow spot between fairly high banks, preferably cutting through a ridge or a mound, high ground that crosses the valley or vale. On the upstream side is a wide depression, at least several feet below the top of the ridge. If you study an aerial photograph of Lake Mead and the Hoover Dam, you will see the same pattern on a massive scale: A location where the minimum amount of dam will create the largest possible lake.

The dam is constructed to a plan, I have read that the beaver begins with a small tree dragged into place, the butt facing downstream. Some dams may be built that way, but this one is not, nor is any other that I have seen. The beaver began

by dropping an eight-inch tree right across the stream. The ends of that tree on land are mostly gone now, but the remnants of the stump prove that the tree was not a random fall. The beaver chewed it down, and dropped it precisely where he wanted it. They can do that, though they are not always successful. This log became a flying foundation for the dam, a foundation on top instead of on the bottom. Perhaps a few vertical supports were added to form a sort of a grate. I have seen just such a structure in other dams, but if they were used here, they are buried in the middle of the mass, well out of sight.

But other logs and thick branches, most likely the largest that the beavers could move, were laid along the front of the foundation and parallel to it, then smaller branches and leaves and mud, more logs, more branches, some at a slant or rising vertically, but most lying horizontal and perpendicular to the dam, thicker  and thicker till the only water passing through was a gentle seepage. The downstream side is reinforced in the same way, small logs, and branches big and small, laid along the dam and then filled in with mud and leaves. Last, the sloping back side was overlaid using heavy branches set vertically, their weight holding the sixty-degree wall in place. This dam was planned, well planned, from lessons learned through long experience, and passed down from one generation to the next.

There is a common phrase, "Busy as a beaver", which is quite apropo, for these beavers have been very busy indeed. There is not simply one dam. There are many. As the waters rose, they found ways around the main dam. Here the beavers

have built smaller dams, and long levees of mud reinforced by bars, by sticks and twigs that spread the load of the weight of water pressing downstream. For it is a very flat land between these confining hills, and thus what would have been a wide meadow bisected by a single stream is instead a series of small, narrow ponds in a long marsh.

For downstream there is another dam, raising a pool to almost the base of the first dam. And below that, a third, a fourth, and more, and more, extending at least a mile down the valley. Some of these dams are small, raising the water only a foot or two. Most are straight, and all are of boughs laid across the stream. One is seven feet wide, but only one foot thick.

This is not merely a dam, this is a project, not merely a beaver dwelling, but a beaver settlement, a village, a town. This is an old complex, begun many years ago, and has certainly been present longer than the lifespan of its originator. Some of the stumps have nearly rotted away, some of the abandoned logs crumble under the weight of a man, and there is nothing at all to indicate that they are detritus of the original construction. And well it should be, for this is prime real estate. Aspen are abundant, a prolific renewable resource, a food supply that can never be exhausted. The water is constant, even in late fall more than enough to maintain the marsh. And the water in the

pools is now deep enough to remain unfrozen in even the coldest winter. And it is hidden. It lies beside a campground, but many the campers do not realize it is there, so well do the lodges blend into the background. I even had one tell me there were no beaver in this forest, while we stood in plain sight of the ponds, and not ten feet from a chewed stump.

I can see the ponds, and the dams, and the stumps, and the debris. But I have never yet seen the beaver. I knew they were here, for several stumps were fresh. When stargazing before moonrise, I remained alert for sounds from the swamp, but the beaver were too elusive. Then, last night, about an hour or two before dawn, I awoke to the cracking of a tree, and heard the trembling crash of its fall. By the time I had escaped from my sleeping bag, the beaver had fled, but fifteen feet from my tent lay a felled aspen. It was only three or four inches in diameter, so I hauled it to the edge of the pond, and apologized to the beaver for disturbing it at its work. The fallen tree had been blocking the road anyway.

No, I have never seen a beaver, not in the wild, only in zoos. Perhaps I never will. I can live with that, content in the certainty that they are there, that we did not kill them all off in the cause of fashion and "gentlemen's" hats. I have never seen a President either, not in real life, not even in a zoo. I might, someday. Though, really, I would rather see a beaver.

Bear Country

There are not many bears in the Rockies. Although Man has encroached heavily on their habitat, that is not the reason there are so few of them; there have always been few. One might think there are a lot, over half a million of them, but not when you consider the size of their territory. Bears are big. They are one of the very, very few animals that are larger than we are. That means they eat a lot of food. Plus, they hibernate for several months each year, living off of their stored fat, which means they eat an especially large amount of food in the Autumn, on the close order of twenty thousand calories each day. (They are highly conscientious weight-watchers. "Honey, do these berries make my butt look fat?" "Yes, dear." "Oh, goodie!") While bears will eat pretty much anything, fish, squirrels, rabbits, deer, berries, nuts, roots, insects, grubs, table scraps, picnic baskets, beer, humans, there is only so much food they can get. They are in competition with all of the other animals in the forests, *all* of them except the pure grazers (as far as I know, bears almost never eat grass), and even the grazers are often food sources. They are most in competition with other bears, so each bear has a territory where no other bears are welcome. They will kill to defend it, and maybe eat the intruder. And that is the limiting factor on bear population. A bear who does not get fat enough will wake from hibernation early, and emerge to a world with very little food available. He is hungry, even desperate, and will happily run down and devour a two-legs, like you or me. And if he is a she with a cub or two (five is not unknown), she is even more fierce. A bear awakened early is at her most dangerous.

As an interesting side note, the sow bear (male bears are boars; female are sows) will be pregnant when she goes into hibernation. She wakes up with a cub or two, because they are born while she sleeps. I expect that makes most of you mothers a bit envious. Actually, hibernation is not exactly *sleep*, but it is close enough for our purposes. The point is, she is extra-hungry because her body has been making milk for the cubs, and now she will have to forage more than usual because she is eating for two or three. So in addition to her strong mother-instinct protectiveness, she is more bad-tempered than the males, and thus even more dangerous. If she thinks there is even a possibility that you might be threatening her cubs, she will attack. If you attract her attention and end up having to kill her, you will be killing her cub (or cubs) as well.

If you are going to venture into Bear Country, even just passing through, you had better learn as much about them as you can, for this is a case where ignorance, which is always fraught with danger, is even more deadly than it usually is. The first rule of Bear Country is, do not be there when the bears are. If you see a bear in the distance, take a picture. If he is closer, say a hundred yards or so, get in your car, or go indoors. If you cannot get to shelter, stand on something, your car or a picnic table or a rock, and look big. Spread your arms. Yell at him. The idea is to make yourself look bigger than him and more dangerous, but not threatening; he will probably go away. Do not run at him; then you look like an enemy, a challenge, and he will likely fight. Do not run away; then you look like prey, and he will probably chase you, and catch you. They can run about thirty miles per hour, even downhill. *You* can *not*. Except maybe downhill. I have a friend who encountered a bear with her cub on a steep mountain trail. Startled, she took a step backwards, which took her off the trail and over the edge. Not a straight drop, it was still steep enough to tumble her a long way before she could stop. It bruised her, it battered her, it scraped and scratched her, and it was the best thing she could have done. If you cannot fall over a cliff, stand still. If the bear comes at you, watch his ears. If they are erect, the bear is bluffing, or still checking you out. He will likely stop short and leave. But if his ears are flattened, he is charging, attacking. He is quite certain: You are lunch. Defend yourself with whatever you have. Even a stick, even a fist, is better than nothing. Or if it is a grizzly, climb a tree, because they cannot climb. Black bears can, and they will come right up after you.

Always carry your defensive weapons where you can get at them instantly. Thirty miles per hour is forty-four feet per second. If the bear is two hundred feet away when he starts his charge, he will reach you in less than five seconds. That is all the time you have to do something. Bear spray, pepper spray, *oleoresin capsicum*, is a popular tool, but not very effective. Four times out of five, it will stop the bear. The other time, it just makes him more angry. A high-voltage zapper, the hand-held device that delivers a hundred-thousand volt charge on contact, is much more effective. I am told that forest and park rangers have taken to carrying them instead of pepper spray. You do not have to hit the bear with it, just click it twice per second as the bear approaches. Apparantly it hurts their ears, very painfully. Some have theorized the ozone smell also contributes, making the bear associate you with lightning, but I doubt that. Whatever the reason it works, it *does* work. I have yet to hear of a single instance of a zapper failing to drive off a bear. It is also effective in scaring off dogs. That I can attest to from personal experience. That is also why I doubt the lightning-smell theory. There was a stone-deaf dog who paid no attention at all. When facing down a bear, I use a zapper and a pistol. Well, I *plan* to use them. I have not yet needed to, not since I learned of the zapper. If the bear gets close enough to terrify me (I will be *scared* from the moment he starts his charge), then I drop the zapper and start shooting for the eyes. It takes a lot of bullet to stop a bear, and few slugs are powerful enough to penetrate the thick skull, but even a .22 will pierce the eye socket and ricochet around inside. I have only had to do that once (and once is more than enough, thank you!), but even that once would not have been necessary if I had understood bears at the time.

The most important point about avoiding bear encounters is to not attract them. They are looking (and smelling) for food. Do not provide it. If you do, if you attract a bear into a campground, the rangers will have to do something about it. Often they can convince a bear to stay away from the campground, but if they cannot, they will either kill the bear, or they will trap it and ship it away to some other forest. That is a sop to the eco-simps, who maintain that relocating the bear is kinder and better than killing it. They are full of what bears do in the woods. Remember territories? There *is* no bear-friendly land that is not already a part of some bear's territory. If we move a stranger into it, the new bear will conflict with the current resident. Either one bear will kill the other, or the weaker will move on. Onto some other bear's land. Eventually, a bear is going to die, killed in battle or starved to death, because one bear was relocated rather than shot. Some kindness! This is why the rangers will tell you "A fed bear is a dead bear".

Anything that smells or looks like it might be food must be locked away, preferably unseeable and unsmellable, but at least unreachable, and *not* in your camp. Locked up in the trunk of your car or inside your RV is best. Next best is a bear locker, a steel box with a latch that bears cannot open. Many campgrounds have them, usually one per campsite. Into those, you put all of your food, even sealed cans and bottles, because many bears have learned that they often contain food, especially beer, and how to get at the food. Also store anything that smells nice, such as soap and perfume, and clothing that you wore while cooking. It smells like food, and bears will come for it. If you cannot lock the food away, hang it from a tree, twelve feet off the ground and four feet from the tree trunk. Pick a tree at least a hundred feet downwind from you, so a bear following the smell will not come through your camp.

Incidentally, these bear-lockers, or at least most that I have seen, can be opened from inside. If you do not have a solid vehicle in which to hide, you might climb into the box and shut it. It will not be comfortable, and the bear may pound on it for a while, but he will not get at you.

Where you camp is also important. I am camped in a beautiful canyon, well over eight thousand feet, surrounded by lush vegetation. A bad wildfire swept through about four years ago, which took out about half of the trees in many places, and all of them in some. But there has been a lot of good rainfall,

especially for the last year with the breaking of the sixty-year-long drought, and the saplings are now emerging to reclaim the land. It is a long time since I have seen a lake full to capacity, as this one is. The brush and grass and other small plants are growing even faster, with their much shorter generations, and succulent roots and berries are abundant. Especially the chokecherry. They are heavy with berries, which

were green when I arrived, but are quickly ripening. Today, or maybe tomorrow, I will be able to pick a gallon of them within fifty feet of my tent. That is, I would if I had any desire to. Chokecherries are edible, and quite tasty, but they are the most astringent food I know of. They are good to toss in a stew, or for flavoring pemmican, but no one would want to eat them like cherries. No one except the bears. And they will. They will come. This is a campground, a busy one. There are a lot of people here, a lot of traffic, but there are also a lot of chokecherries, and the bears know it. They will come.

Remember the first rule of Bear Country? So do I. I will be leaving first thing in the morning.

Bear's Tepee
National Monument

Bear in the Tent

Now, you should know by this time what to do about bears. Like do not be too close, mostly by not attracting them. If you are too close, do not appear threatening, and do not appear appetizing, or even weak, and at the same time, try to convince them that you are dangerous, but perfectly willing to let them get away with it this time, as long as they leave you alone. Do not run, do not charge, but do look big and powerful. And loud. But also be ready to carry out the threat if they decide you are bluffing. Carry bear spray or a high-voltage zapper, and a gun. Of course you do not *want* to kill it, or even bother it, but even less do you want to be killed yourself. Never forget, like it or not you are betting your life, here, so always be ready, just in case.

I was in Bear Country at the time. It was a well-supplied campground, with bear-proof lockers, and fewer than a dozen campsites, so there was less chance of an ignorant camper leaving out enticing treats. My food and tasty-smelling stuff was all packed away in the locker; a bear could probably still smell some of it, because those lockers are not airtight, but, then, there was not much to smell. My zapper and pistol lay beside a flashlight within reach of my bed, where I could almost instantly lay hands on them. About the only further preparation I could have made would have been to be someplace else. But this time, it was not enough.

The weather was warm, and the nights pleasantly cool. In fact, I would have been sleeping outside, except there was a fair chance of thunderstorms this night. As it was, my curtains were open and the door as well, allowing the scented night breezes to waft through the tent. They also enabled a bear to enter without tearing through the canvas. But the odds against a bear appearing were high, and there was no way to be one hundred percent secure. I had taken all of the precautions I reasonably could, and was satisfied with them. Until I was awakened sometime after midnight, most likely by the quiet rustling of the bear's movements. The night was starlit, though moonless, but even so I did not see him, nor did I sense his bulk, but knew there was something there, a Presence. I silently picked up my zapper and flashlight, aimed, and illuminated the area. And there it was, big as life, crouched on the floor: a full-grown bear. I was looking right into his bright, beady eyes, his black nose and sharp white teeth not two feet from me. I was wrapped in my sleeping bag. It was not zipped up, the night being too warm, but I was lying on it, so I could not throw it to confuse the critter. My second bag, used as a blanket on top, was cast aside, well out of reach. I had nothing but the zapper and my wits, there being no time to switch to the pistol. I stared at the bear, waiting, quite willing to let him leave peacefully. He stared back, unblinking.

It turned out I had made a mistake, a small one, but a mistake nonetheless: I had eaten some cookies as a bedtime snack, and there were a few crumbs on the floor. That is what attracted him. Sure, they were small, tiny, in fact, but the scent was present. Enough, clearly, to attract the scavenger. He had been nibbling at them when my light took him by surprise. I stared, he stared. I waited, he waited. He was recovering from the shock and trying to decide what to do. The zapper was armed, the red ready light glowing, but I did not want to trigger it. They high-pitched crackling sound it produces is supposed to hurt the ears of animals, making them run away at once; it works on dogs, squirrels and racoons, but I had never had a need, or chance, to try it on anything else. If the bear was confused and thought he was trapped, well, any cornered animal, however small, will fight if he thinks he has no other choice. I was hoping he would decide the scanty meal was not worth any risk. He could not see me through the flashlight's glare, but he knew I was there, he knew what I was. He had known before he entered, for he could smell me, even though I had had a bath that day. All animals know the smell of a two-legs, and usually fear it, or at least respect it. Did this one? What experience did he have with two-legs? Was he hungry enough, bold enough, to think of me as breakfast?

He decided and acted. With a quick flash of gray-brown fur, he squeaked, dashed out the door and vanished in the grass. I was safe. I relaxed.

On later reflection, I do not believe I was ever in any great danger. Perhaps the few tiny crumbs he had eaten before I awoke had been enough to satisfy him. Full-grown though he was, he could not have been over two inches long, plus another three for his tail.

Bah!

There is a lot of wildlife residing in the area. Besides the ever-present chipmunks and squirrels and robins and sparrows, I have seen cranes and eagles, moose, elk, and especially deer. They appear in much greater abundance than they did in any prior year, which lavish presence I attribute to the lushness of the flora, rather than any increase in population. And today I saw a new one, an animal I had never seen in this area, though I had seen signs of them, scat and spoor. And not just one. Hundreds, thousands, all at once.

The invasion began. . . No, I should not call it an invasion. The poor creatures had no desire to come here. They were driven, they were refugees, they were fleeing a pack of carnivores nipping at their heels, chivvying them along. The animals were crying out in fear and distress, pursued through the trees and chased along the creek, driven from behind and herded from the sides, till they entered a vast meadow, rich with green grass and thick bracken. And there they stopped, for their persecutors no longer drove them. Indeed, a pair of pursuers had run ahead and barred their further passage. The recently frightened flock ceased their stampede and settled in to graze, behaving exactly like a flock of domesticated sheep, which is a good thing, because that is exactly what they were.

Now, everybody knows that sheep are slow and stupid. Domesticated sheep, that is. Wild sheep, bighorns, well, they are a different animal entirely. Hollywood, Disney, even George Orwell, painted a very dim image of sheep. And for once, they got it right. Even Disney. The sheep *is* a very dim animal. The rapidity with which the flock calmed down and began to feed clearly demonstrated how short their attention span is. There is a dirt road through the meadow, a popular route for campers on ATVs. Sheep on the road would scramble off as the vehicle approached, but the ones on the roadsides generally did not run away till after the ATV had passed. This shows how long it takes for an idea, or what passes for an idea, to penetrate their understanding. Most probably because their understanding is so small, it takes the idea a very long time to locate it. Sheep make squirrels seem intelligent!

The carnivores controlling the flock look like dogs, but they are in fact Sheep Guardians. Apparantly the Political Correctness dupes believe the term "sheepdog" is derogatory, and they fear to offend the critters. I can understand the fear. The dogs know their business, and are quite ready to face down and even attack anything they suspect may be threatening their charges. And they are very intelligent, much smarter than the PC dupes. There is a barbed wire fence between the meadow and the creek. I watched a sheepdog patrol the creek side to see if any sheep had managed to get through, then *climb* over, not crawl under, not jump, not even scramble, but *climb over* the fence. Very impressive! "Guardian" is not an appropriate title for these dogs. They do guard the sheep (though I doubt the wool-heads see it that way), but they do so much more! "Sheep controller" might do, but their traditional name of "sheepdog" says it all. I watched them, off and on, all day. I saw many sheep, thousands in the flock, but only a half dozen dogs, and no one else. No shepherds. Why were there no shepherds? Because the sheepdogs did not need them.

Or it could be because there no longer are any shepherds. Instead, there are Sheep Operators. I am not making this up. It is true! The Government says so. There is a big sign by the road in the middle of the field warning that Sheep Operators use Sheep Guardians, and that you should not approach the sheep, and especially not the Guardians. Back away. Say "No!" or "Go back!" I doubt this is good advice. Most of the shepherds in this area are from South America. They may speak English (and may not), but sure as certain, they train their dogs in Spanish. Or maybe Portuguese. It is a safe bet that no bureaucrat, or anyone else, consulted with any shepherd when composing that sign.

"Sheep Operator." Whose idiotic idea was that? Did some one actually think shepherds were insulted or felt degraded by the title? Not a chance, bucko! They are proud of it! Hey, how about "cowboy"? Did you know it originally meant "rustler"? How is *that* for offensive? And how do you think today's cowboys would react if some nitwit decided to relable them "Cattle Operators"? May the Good Sheep Operator have mercy on anyone who tries!

I hope that last sentence did not offend you. Unless you are a PC Promoter, in which case I hope it did. It is just that "sheep operator" sounds sort of obscene. I picture some jerk in a truck festooned with antennas, sitting before a control panel so complex it would be a NASA Flight Controller's nightmare, or a Hollywood Prop Artist's wet-dream. He pushes buttons and flips switches to make the sheep move or graze, to go out in the fields in the morning and return to the fold at night. Granted, the sheep need that kind of control, given that one can eat all the grass in front of it, then starve before it figures out that if it takes a few steps, it will reach more grass. But the sheepdogs supply all of the needed control quite well, thank you. They know exactly how to push the sheep's buttons.

I never before had an opportunity such as this to study sheep. Some of my relatives, farmers in Illinois, had a few dozen sheep, so I became acquainted with them on summer visits. But I was not much interested, and paid them little attention. I have often seen flocks in the fields while riding by, but not close up. Today I had a chance to sit by the flock and just watch them. Their migration path is only fifty yards from my campsite. So, for the first time, I paid attention to sheep. I watched them. I *looked* at them.

I had heard that very close to one in each hundred sheep is not white. By my observation, it is true. I used to wonder why black and brown sheep were tolerated; surely their wool is worth much less than that of white sheep. Then I was told that shepherds do not count their sheep. They count the brown and black ones, and multiply by one hundred. Clever. Simple, and obvious (at least, now that I have told you), but clever. No sheep could have figured that out. Or bureaucrat.

The End

There is a pronghorn antelope in the park. The ranger tells me it is the first one ever sighted here, at least since the area was established as a state park. I must have looked doubtful, as the land is excellent grazing ground for antelope, and pronghorns, too. (Oh, sorry, I should point out that the pronghorn is not actually an antelope, any more than the prairie dog is a dog. Relatively ignorant pioneers and settlers named a lot of things for what was familiar, and scientific taxonomy was decidedly *not* familiar.) They also are herd beasts; I have never seen a lone one. Maybe as few as four or five, but not just one. Before I could comment, the ranger noted that in spite of being a state park, the land was still open range, and ranchers were accustomed to letting their cattle roam it. Fair enough. You need about a hundred acres of this kind of land to raise one cow. That is a lot of competition for the pronghorns.

I set off with camera and binoculars to see if I could spot the beast. Sure, it was a long shot, but I had nothing better to do, nothing at all. This desert prairie is beautiful land, if you know how to look at it, and wandering through it looking is a fine way to spend a few hours. "Barren wasteland." "Arid scrub." "Worthless desert." City folks have many names for this kind of land. That is okay; we have many names for them, too. There are a great many animals living in this lifeless land, and the barren soil is half-covered (well, at least a third) by grass and bush and scrub. Very little cactus; I have hardly seen any, yet. The animals have not been very visible these last few days, because the wind has been quite strong. I suppose the little animals find it scary; they cannot hear an approaching predator when the wind is rustling the grass and whushing through the brush. The shadows of the waving branches must also be disturbing, since a moving shadow generally means a hawk of some sort. All big birds are hawks to the ground squirrels and field mice; better to hide from everything than make a (fatal) mistake. But even the raptors are rare, as fifty mile per hour gusts make soaring difficult. The animals know about fire, and fear it. The smell of smoke means danger. About twenty or thirty miles to the South, a wildfire is raging through the pines. No one does more than dream about controlling it, not in this wind and the extreme dryness of . . . everything! But the fire is directly upwind, and the smoke fills the air with a pale, thin, slightly brown haze. In the late afternoon, it is a brown cloud that reddens the sunlight. The smell is present at all times. The tiny prey critters must be near a state of nervous exhaustion. Better to stay in their dens and eat what stored food they may have. Or go hungry.

Still, there are a few about, and beetles clinging to the stems, and sparrows or finches or something dodging along the ground to hunt them. I saw a couple of ground mammals, just glimpses, not enough to identify them, and a few ravens. No coyotes, snakes, or lizards, but several tracks. And finally, there, far off in the distance, something. I set my binoculars on the monopod, and cranked up the magnification (can't do that without a support). At full eighty power I could see it was the pronghorn. Half the time the image was dancing around, but it held steadily enough for long enough to get a good look. Big fellow, but rather ratty and grizzled. Thin, I could easily see ribs. And he seemed to have a limp. I tried to get closer, into camera range, but he knew I was there, and wanted nothing to do with me. He did not run or bound as pronghorns so joyfully do. He just limped along, glancing back now and then. Then I knew. He is old, weak, maybe sick. That is why he is alone. He cannot keep up with the others, and they dare not lag behind when danger threatens.

Now, there are some who would try to help, bring him food and water. But even if they could get their CARE packages close enough to him, they would be doing him no favor. He would be like those poor wretches in hospitals, incurable, certain to die, no possibility of recovery, but being kept alive by fabulously expensive machines, burning through insurance and savings and amassing huge debts for their families. All for a few more days of life. Pain-wracked, drug-dazed, half aware (if that much), suffering for another day. Is death so frightening that we must torture ourselves to avoid it? Some day, very soon, this old pronghorn will die. Maybe he will just not awake in the morning. Maybe the coyotes will find him some night, and pull him down. I am rather surprised they have not already done so. But it is okay. It is all right. He has had a long and full life. As big as he is, as strong as he must once have been, he undoubtedly leaves scores of descendants. And with the weather as it is, the coyotes need a good feed. Let it go. It is time.

I kept an eye out after that, whenever I was walking across the prairie, but I never saw the old fellow again. The rangers did, a day or two after my encounter. They usually check out gatherings of buzzards and vultures, on the off chance it is a human in dire straits. They found the body, what was left of it. They could not tell how he had died, but the coyotes had eaten most of the flesh, and cracked the bones for marrow. Ravens and other scavengers were pecking off what was left, and ants were gleaning the bits no one else could reach. Mice and bacteria and weather will eventually crumble the bones, and in a year or so, there will be no trace left, except perhaps an exceptionally rich patch of grass.

That is how I want to go. No locking up the body in a plastic box and burying it in some wasteful cemetary. Embalming and burial is sinful, or at least selfish (but, then, is there a difference?) Locking away all of these nutrients, taking the body out of the circle of life for thousands of years at the least. Cremation is almost as bad, burning the body to basic elements, but at least the elements return to the ecosystem. Many of the Indians had the right idea, exposing the bodies of their dead on platforms, food for the scavengers and raptors. They had taken sustenance from the world, and then they gave it back. I would ask that my body be deposited somewhere in the Wilds, to let the flesh be devoured and the bones moulder back to the soil. But the Law will not allow it. It is unsanitary. Maybe, when I am near my last legs, I might trade my bike for a ride into the deep mountains, then walk as far as I can. And when the time is right, when I can go no farther, when I find a suitable spot, light a stick of dynamite, and curl up on top of it. Blow the body into so many fragments, they will never find more than a few pounds. The rest will stay, as birds and beasts and bugs and brush. And maybe next lifetime, I may return with my new body and sit in a small glade, fertilized by my old corpse, and pick up where I left off. That is Heaven.

Squish!

I set out for town this morning on a very important errand: I wanted ice cream. It is only a dozen miles, through pine-filled canyons and over spreading grassy meadows and past a rustic village nestled on the shores of a clear blue lake. The road is paved the whole way, with long grass on the verges.

As I approached, a ground squirrel sped out of the shelter on the far side, his course and speed precisely correct to place the furry streak exactly in front of my tire at the very instant I arrived there. But he never made it. From the other direction came a pickup truck. The squirrel passed well in front of the right tire and continued with unaltered speed, and met the left tire dead center, his head and front paws on one side, tail and hind legs on the other. Blood and guts spurted from both ends, and the flattened corpse did a flip in the air and straddled the center line.

Why do they do it? It is not a rare event. I know one campground that is approached by a two-mile road that goes nowhere else. Every morning there are six or eight fresh pieces of roadkill, each attended by three or four ravens. Every single morning. Six per day for a whole year means two thousand one hundred ninety squashed squirrels. There must be a huge rodent population around there.

Most roadkill I can understand. Possums and porcupines, turtles and skunks, slow critters that could not get out of the way however smart they might be, however hard they might try. Any collision at night, when the animal, already in the middle of the road, stunned by the sudden light, freezes in place, unable to think, uncomprehending of what is happening, unknowing of what it should do, unaware of whether it can do anything or not, is perfectly understandable, and something that drivers should expect and be constantly alert for. In Idaho, such occurences are so common, the locals weld heavy grates on the fronts of their vehicles. Not for those little fellows, the squirrels and rabbits and slow-moving nocturnals; deer, elk, and especially moose are so big, they can total a car in one lethal collision. Flash! Thump! Game over. Often driver over, too.

That is at night. A blinding, brilliant blaze, as bright as the sun, in the middle of the night. Of course it confuses the little animals! Of course they cannot react! It is like walking down a city street and getting hit on the head with a falling brick. No one expects it, and even if they saw it coming, most people would not think to duck or step aside in time.

But I am not talking about night, or blinding light, or a sudden and unexpected event. Daytime. Straight road. The vehicle can be seen and heard several hundred feet away. And the resident varmint has surely seen these monsters before. Dozens, hundreds of them have been observed passing in the past, and never, never has a single one left that hard black trail. I saw a turkey, once, a couple hundred yards ahead on a divided highway. He saw me, and darted across the pavement long before I could arrive. He crossed the divider. He waited as he watched two cars go by, then, with a long and empty stretch in sight, dashed across the rest of the road. He knew what he was doing. He had figured it out. He understood. Why don't the squirrels and the rabbits? Are they like the lemmings, suicidal maniacs eager to hurl themselves from cliffs, or swim into the sea till they sink? No, not even lemmings do that. It is a myth, a Disney lie that originated in a faked documentary in the 1950s. Are they like the tiny field mice, who cower, confused by an owl's hoot, unable to figure out where it is coming from, or how far away it is? Do they freeze in fear, panic building till they can stand it no longer, and they break from cover in a desperate effort to get away from the dreadful place that scares them so?

Probably.

I expect most of them head away from the road, but we rarely see those, so we take no notice. It is like the reason it always rains just when you do not want it to, or why campfire smoke always follows you around wherever you move. They do not. You only pay attention when they are annoying, and do not even notice the other times. The squirrels and rabbits that we do see dash straight across, the shortest possible distance to desired safety. Also the shortest possible distance to dire disaster. Sometimes they freeze in the middle of the road. Sometimes they are already there when we abruptly appear around a blind curve. And if they are just sitting there, that is all they do: Sit there. Right up to the last possible fraction of a second. Then they leap, but you never know in advance which way they will jump. You do know they will jump, but it is a fifty-fifty chance that they will launch themselves directly into your path.

So what can you do? I slow down as quickly as I can safely do so. I am not sure that makes any difference, but it is a good reflex to have for those times when the target is a deer instead of a squirrel. The tactic proved itself recently when I rounded the curve of a forest road and saw four deer to one side. I was only doing thirty-five, in a fifty-five zone, because I knew there were deer present. I braked as hard as I could without skidding, but was too close to stop in time. The first doe started a dash across the road, and the two fawns and other doe followed in line. The fawns only followed the lead doe, not thinking, just reacting. The last doe hesitated at my slow approach, opening a narrow gap to the last fawn. I slipped through doing no more then ten MPH. The doe stared after me, then leapt in panic at the sound of screeching tires from the following pickup truck. If I had not been there, I expect that truck would have killed a deer or two.

But that is deer. One must dodge around them. For a little fellow, after I start slowing, I aim straight for him. If he does not move, he is dead-dead-dead! But he does move, always. Maybe forwards, maybe back, but whichever way he jumps, I will miss him. Back when I tried to miss them, I hit them instead, all too often. But since I started aiming for them, I have not hit a single one. Not one.

The ravens are not very happy about that.

You do not really
want a photo of
roadkill, do you?

Vole

Coyotes will readily rip apart trash bags to get at food scraps, scattering debris which the wind will then spread over several acres. To avoid this, I do not put edibles in the trash. This is La Posa, the burning plateau named for the toll of the funeral bell, where the wanderers, the residents of the road, gather in their RVs and wait out the winter. Over a million of these snowbirds flock here each year, and these animals have grown accustomed to snatching human food as a normal part of their meager winter diet; like the citizens of the nearby town of Quartzsite, they glean what they can from the transients, and live on it for the rest of the year. So I scatter the scraps around the pole where hangs the hummingbird feeder, a dole for the poor of my parish. The roadrunners and the coyotes gobble the gobbets of beef and chicken and bass and sole and catfish, Rabbits nibble on nubs of carrots and on wilted lettuce and cabbage leaves. The birds and ground squirrels grab the crumbs and fragments of bread and rolls in preference to scavenging snacks from the seed-bolls on the brush.

Striped ground squirrels used to abound in this area, but for some reason they have become few. I have seen only three this winter, a mated pair and what I should expect is their sole remaining foal, or kitten, or whatever they are called, from their last litter. Coyotes seem more abundant, which may explain the absence of their favored prey, though the mice seem especially numerous. But in addition to Stripey and his mate and progeny, there is a newcomer, a species I had not seen before. A bit smaller, with a less-bushy tail, a sharper snout, and no stripes. He is a Mexican vole, just recently released from the Endangered Species list. He has no greens-card, and must compete with the local rodents for what little food there is. His beady eyes are as black as coal or as the kohl with which Egyptians darkened their eyelids, He wears a stole of desert tan, a fine fur that just begs to be stroked. But that will never be, for he watches me as the police watch an ax-murderer on parole. While I may be his *maitre de* when I am sitting still, the moment I move I transform into a troll, a fee-fi-fole giant scenting the blood of a Mexican vole, and he is off like an all-terrain rocket the moment he sees me twitch or feels the ground vibrate under the sole of my shoe.

I must extol his remarkable intelligence. Being smaller than the resident ground squirrels, he would generally have to flee whenever Stripey appeared. Knowing this, he would slip in when the other was not near, steal the larger fragments of rolls, carry them to a mouse-hole a dozen feet away, and stash them therein. Then, when the "rightful" owner appeared, the vole would spend his time moving the stolen rolls from his stash to his own hole fifteen yards away. It was not even his main hole. That was a good ten yards farther, under the bole of a bush on a small knoll on the far side of a dirt road. When I first arrived, and the food scraps began appearing, he had crossed the whole deadly distance, dodging hawks and ATVs, then scrambling for what scraps he could get before Stripey showed up. When he failed to make an appearance for over a week, I assumed his luck had run out, that he had paid the toll required of tiny rodents in the desert, and one of the hawks had found a meal. But he returned; he had spent the time digging, like a mole, a new tunnel under the road!

But when I broke my parole and switched to my troll role, at the very first toll of my sole on my stroll to the pole, the timid soul stole a sole roll from the dole bowl, to bowl a droll roll the whole way to his goal, and loll in the little vole mole-hole under the bole on the knoll.

Six-Legs

Crickets

I would be surprised to meet a person who has never heard crickets. I have heard them everywhere from desert to sub-alpine montane, in country and city, even once on a yacht in the middle of the Caribbean Sea. But I would also be surprised (and gratified) to meet a person who has *listened* to crickets. People hear a chirp, and recognize it as coming from a cricket. They are aware of the sound, they are aware of the fact that they have recognized and labelled it, but they do not pay any attention to the sound. *Do you hear that?* Yeah, it's a cricket. *Listen to it.* Yeah, I'm listening. *What do you hear?* A cricket. *What does it sound like?* A cricket! Wanna beer?

I have heard many lone crickets, and often heard a dozen or more. Sometimes, such as last night, I have heard hundreds, maybe thousands, all at once, not a concert but a cacophony. They seem to follow a pattern, but it changes, for it is actually many patterns, not quite synchronized with each other. The tempo of their chirps increases as they grow warmer. One can even calculate the temperature by timing their chirps. This means the crickets in the cooler areas will be singing slightly slower than the ones in the warmer spaces, and their songs will then overlap in a gradually changing pattern. The bigger and stronger ones will also be louder and have a lower note, for what we call a chirp is really stridulation, the vibration from rubbing their long hind legs on their wing cases. The male crickets are calling for a mate. "Hey, baby, I'm the biggest bug around. Why waste your time with those larvae? Come on over to my place."

I lay under the stars enthralled by the massed pick-up lines. One stood out, loud and distinct, calling his four-beat da-da-da-dum, three notes the same, followed by one higher note. (Beethoven made the fourth note lower, and won eternal fame. Poor crickets!) I suppose the loud one was closer than the others, and warmer, for the chorus slowly fell behind. His chirp was very fast, sort of Mexican, with the Rs rolled. It was difficult to distinguish each click, for the chirp was almost a buzz, and required great concentration to count them. The crickets' night on the forest lasted more than two hours, subtly slowing as the night air cooled, gradually diminishing as the lucky ones picked up dates. The bold one stopped abruptly, hopefully because he was found by a female, and not rolled by a predator. Such is life. Or death.

I listened to the rhythms slowly flowing in a sort of super-syncopation, reinforcing and counter-pointing each other, sometimes blending and rising like a rogue wave at sea to tower together in a crescendo of unity that lasts only a second before dissolving into a buzz of randomity, a sonic brownian motion shoving the rhythm in every possible direction. It is spell-binding. Perhaps some genius musician will listen to their symphony and master it, deriving a new music, a new artform, based not on tone but on interaction of rhythm. Ah, where is Lennon when I need him?

The sound is strongly soothing. It is neither soft nor gentle, and yet, it seems to say "Safety!" I feel it is like the fascination of fire, hearkening back thousands and millions of years, to ages when Man and his ancestors were stalked by creatures terribly more threatening than any that survive today, when we had only sticks and stones to break their bones, and words we hoped would hurt them. I have walked night fields noisy with crickets, and always they fall silent at my approach.

So long as they blithely call, I know no predator approaches, no stealthy bogey sneaks up on me. These crickets are my watchdogs, who bark only in the absence of alarm, sentries calling that all is well. I can relax, and sleep in peace.

Sometime after I fell asleep, "Last orders" was called, for when I awoke, the dawn was chill, the silence complete, save for the tiniest hint of a small brook. It, too, will cease singing when the weather cools enough, but only a hard freeze will suffice to silence it. The day is warming slowly, for it is now September at six thousand feet, and the sky is solid overcast. No crickets sing, for the day-birds are hunting. I rather miss their sound. I think tonight, if it does not rain, I shall have a campfire, and see if the flames dance in rhythm to the insects' love song. I bet they will.

Beetle Behavior

It is a very pretty beetle, with a sort of diamond shaped, light chocolate brown body. If you took a Christian cross and drew lines to connect the four ends, that is the shape of its body, more or less. I never saw one of this species before, which is not at all surprising, as I am told there are more than three hundred thousand beetle species described. So far. That is more than all of the other non-insect macroscopic species put together. It has the usual six legs and two antennae, and at least two pairs of wings tucked invisibly under its wing cases.

I first saw it earlier today, when it was crawling along the table. I was preparing chile at the time, and did not want to mix the bug in. Not unless I was making ooey-gooey creepy-crawly stew, which I decidedly was not. So I gently, softly flicked it off. It swiftly spread its wings and drifted to a light landing. Now, half a day later, sitting in the shade of a warm afternoon, digesting a fine bellyful of really good chile and watching my favorite reality show (which is whatever may drift by my campsite), who should stroll by but that same beetle. Or maybe it is its brother. Or uncle. Or third cousin twice removed on its mother's side. I do not like to sound like a bigot, but if I want to be honest, I must admit that all beetles of a given species look pretty much the same to me. Anyway, it passes a couple feet from me and proceeds to wander across a bare stretch of dirt, broken only by a few twigs, a few more pebbles, and a red plastic-sheathed extension cord. It ambles along in no particular direction, on a more or less straight line, in no discernable hurry, steadfastly going over anything smaller than itself, and patiently going around anything larger. When it has to detour, though, it always comes back to the same course as it had started on, as if it has a specific destination in mind.

Beetles are really fascinating to watch. Their method of motion is actually quite sophisticated. Although they have six legs, they walk in a two-step. They lift the front and back legs on one side, and the middle leg on the other side, move them forward, and set them down. Then they raise the other three legs and move them in the same way. Thus they are always suspended on a stable tripod, and do not have to spend a lot of brain-power, which they do not have in the first place, on figuring out which leg to move next. Not like that old joke about the centipede who, when asked how he knew which leg to move, got so confused he never walked again. (Whoever made that joke had never watched a centipede; their legs flow in a wave motion, much like the teeth of a comb move when you run your fingernail along them.) Most beetles wave their antennae, or feelers, in front of them, one going up while the other goes down. They are held in a slightly spread position, so they are "feeling" the area they are about to walk through. Using this technique, if such a bug should come to a barrier that has a hole of just the right size for the bug to walk through, it could do so without ever touching the sides or roof of the tunnel, and probably would.

My little visitor crosses the terrain slowly, steadily and purposefully till it comes to the extension cord. Now this is apparently something new to it. It is shaped sort of like a twig, but much smoother, and must be harder to get a grip on. But a long reach is enough to procure a sort of a grip on the top, and the beetle hoists itself up, where it pauses to wave its antennae around and feel nothing, then steps forward, falls off, and lands upside down on the ground. It waves its legs around for a few seconds and finally manages to touch something and get just enough leverage to flip over. It then continues on exactly the same course as it had started. Now, how does it know that? What is it orienting itself on? The Earth's magnetic field? Not the sun, for it is in solid shadow. Not on any landmark ahead of it, for beetle eyes cannot distinguish anything so vastly far off (like, say, two feet). However it may manage the trick, it does continue forward, but as ill luck would have it, the cord lies in a loop, and crosses the beetle's projected path twice more. When it again reaches a length of cord, it repeats the first encounter in minute detail: A few swipes at the surface, a long reach, grip, hoist, pause, wave, step . . . and fall on its back. A bit of waving and a flip, and it is back on course following the same magnetic force line or whatever. A few more inches of plodding along bring it to the third bit of cord, where it nonchalantly steps through the *exact – same – motions*, no slightest variation, no hesitation, no visible trepidation or anticipation of the fall. Is this fool bug incapable of learning? Is its attention span so short that it does not even remember the earlier crossings? Or is it satisfied with the procedure, since it does come out at the end unharmed, undamaged and successfully past the barrier? Who knows what goes through the mind of an insect, assuming it has a mind for something to go through?

The tiny acrobat proceeds on its seemingly inevitable straight line till it comes to a gigantic rock, fifty times its height and ten times its length – that is to say, five inches high and seven inches long. There it pauses and waits, I do not think even it knows what for, then eventually turns right. But at the end of the rock, instead of turning back to its beloved straight course, goes on another three inches to a small pile of tiny dead flowers fallen from a nearby tree. It walks into the middle of this two-inch slash pile and stops. And sits there. Just sits there. Maybe it found a snack. Maybe it is just comfortable. From a far distant (on a bug's scale) six feet away, I can discern no activity at all. And the longer I look, the harder it is to see the beetle, for its color is precisely that of the micro-woodpile it rests on. I glance away for a moment, and when I look back, can not find it. It could not have moved away, could not even have flown away, not in the two seconds my gaze was averted, not at the speeds it could manage. I stare for over a minute, and can not make it out until it finally begins moving again. Such magnificently good camouflage! I knew it was there, I knew its exact shape, size, color and position, but I *still* could not see it till it moved. It wanders off, not on its original magnetic line, but on the same course that had led from the rock to the flowers. Perhaps it was reasoning (if you will allow me the use of the word) that this course had brought it to food (assuming the stop *had* been occasioned by the finding of food), so continuing the course might bring it to more food. The old course had, after all, brought it nothing but three tumbles and an impassable barrier. Whatever the reason, the beetle proceeds unimpeded, for there are no more barriers or bouquets in its path, till it reaches a stand of green grass, and vanishes into its unplumbed depths, never more to be seen.

And then another one, half the size of the first, perhaps a grand niece or great nephew, emerges from the same place as the original, following the same magically marked trail, right up to the extension cord. This one, at half the size of the first, has a much harder time scaling the undercut cliff and getting a grip on the smoothly curved upper surface. But it does not carefully tumble over the side. No, this one turns and marches along the length of the cord, staying on top, following the curves, five feet, ten feet, twenty feet, speeding along the

Interstem Freeway at seventy-five feet per hour till it reaches an exit offering grass, food and lodging. The same clump of grass, oddly enough, into which the first beetle disappeared.

Why they behaved so differently, I do not know. There is no doubt they were the exact same species. They were of a different generation, maybe different sex, but they surely must have had extremely similar needs and motivations. Perhaps the older one had prior experience with extension cords. This is, after all, a popular campground. Perhaps there is a logical and obvious reason which I can never comprehend, insects being so dramatically alien to mammals. I watched for a while, hoping for a third beetle to traipse by, giving me more data to work with, but it never came.

Perhaps it flew by overhead while I was looking down.

Moths

Most people know butterflies. Most people like them, even love them. I do not know anyone who dislikes them, or is even bothered by them. They frolic throughout the day, over and in gardens and meadows and forests, flitting on drunken erratic sprawls going from nowhere to anywhere, randomly roaming wherever any giddy puff of breeze blows, alighting on any blossom or blade that may present itself. Wearing any and all colors, from the purest white to deepest black,and the entire rainbow and more between, seeming to display more colors than exist, sometimes striving to include all of them onto a single wing. They are an internationally known symbol of beauty. And yet, they are only a minor mutation of the moth.

The moth is one of the most magnificent creations ever to have existed. There are some quarter million species that we know about, each bearing six legs, four wings, and a pair of fuzzy feelers, but with almost every imaginable variation of shape and color. A few hold their wings constantly erect. Most fold them in some fashion. Some wear camouflage that makes them disappear in their normal environment; some others bear the most brilliant colors starkly contasting against literally any background. For most of their lives, they are not even moths, but caterpillars or cocoons. Some of them never eat again, once they enter their cocoon.

On emergence, they mate and lay eggs within a day, then retire and spend the next week or so flitting from camp to camp, wandering where they will, with no duties, no obligations, their tasks accomplished, their purposes fulfilled. Now they play until they are prey, or exhaust their stored food supply.

Most live for several weeks as moths, some breeding repeatedly during this time. These are not the ones who strip trees of their leaves, or who get into your closets and drawers and chew holes in your favorite clothes. These are the ones who are a mainstay of our great eco-systems. A few years ago, some simpletons found out that many bee-keepers were losing half of their broods. Not realizing that this is a normal and somewhat cyclic phenomenon, these fools decided pesticides must be to blame, and pounced, screaming "Oh! Oh! Oh! *All* of the bees are going extinct, and then all pollinization will cease, and all of our food crops will fail, and all flowers will vanish forever!" As a matter of fact, only the domesticated European honeybee was involved, and not any of the vastly greater numbers of native bees that inhabit our forests and fields and croplands. If all of the domestic bees died, the bee-keepers would go out of business, and honey would become more expensive, but there would be little or no other significant effect. But what if *all* of the bees *did* disappear? What would happen then? Nothing much. Somewhere around four fifths of all pollination is accomplished by - - - moths. What? How can that be? We see lots of bees, but never many moths!

The answer is, almost all moths are nocturnal. Some quiet, clear night, take a powerful flashlight and point it upward. More often than not, you will see myriad moths flicking through the beam. Or get a set of night-vision goggles or binoculars and gaze out on a moonless or moonlit landscape. You will see countless scintillating spots of pale light flitting any and everywhere amongst the grasses and bushes and trees. Millions of them, all night long, swarms of fairies frisking among the moonbeams.   Larger shapes swoop through the swarms like dolphins through baitballs; bats are feasting on their main food source.   You want to see bats?   This is the surest way, save for standing outside their caves and shelters as they emerge at dusk.

Moths do a little damage, chewing holes in our woolens. They can be somewhat annoying, swarming around our lights at night.   But that is our fault, for having the light out there. Moths navigate by the moon, a bright and stable beacon.   They "know" that if they keep the Moon in the same position relative to themselves, they will be flying in a pretty straight line. Smart.   But they cannot tell the difference between the Moon and a light bulb or a candle flame.   Try it yourself.   Walk with the Moon ahead of you and a little to the left.   If you keep the Moon in the same position, you will walk in a straight line. Now do the same with a streetlamp or a campfire.   You will spiral around it, getting closer and closer, till you walk right into it.   Same thing with moths, except that you will stop before treading into the fire, because you know the Moon does not radiate heat.   The moths have not figured that out, and the fuddled insect ends up spiralling in until it bounces off of the light, or fries in the flame.   They are not *attracted* to the light; they just do not expect it to be so close.

Moths are also an excellent food source.   In a survival situation, you can quickly gather a quart or two with nothing but a light and a fine net.   They are quite good when roasted, and have a delicate crunchiness.   The taste reminds me of wild hickory nuts.

Butterflies

People talk about making a bee-line to something, meaning to go utterly straight. Personally, I have never seen a bee fly in a straight line for more than a few inches. They will wander and swerve and dip and rise and manage to travel in every direction possible while traversing a mere ten feet. Even when heading back to the hive, they look like they are being buffeted by a gusty wind. The only way that their flight can be considered straight is by comparison with the path of a butterfly.

Have you ever watched the flight of a butterfly? Really watched it, not just seen it happen? Its flight path is as erratic as the scribbles of a child with his very first crayon. It is utterly unpredictable. Utterly. You cannot even count on the path trending in any general direction. I suspect even the butterfly has no idea where it is going. It flaps its wings and blithers about till it runs into something, then grabs on and checks to see if it is a flower, or maybe another butterfly of the opposite sex. If not, it starts flapping again, and repeats the process till it finds something to eat. For that matter, some of them do not eat, and only reproduce immediately after they emerge from the chrysalis. Where are these going? What are they doing? Are they retired, and just having a good time? I have heard about the Monarch butterflies migrating in great swarms. I have never seen it myself, but would dearly love to do so. Huge clouds of a million monarchs drift along, moving in a steady direction, but internally, a random mess, individuals moving in every direction, colliding with each other, popping out of the cloud and dropping back in. It must be beautiful.

Butterflies are actually a variety of moth, and a fairly recent one at that, their relationship somewhat similar to that of humans to apes. The butterflies have lost the feathery part of the feelers, and the ability to fold their wings, and apparantly all of the aeronautic and navigational skills as well, along with what little intelligence the moths may have. Moths tend to be rather dull, wearing muted shades of gray and brown. Some clearly resemble the rocks and trees of their environs, which effectively hides them from predatory birds. Sometimes. If they do not move. Mostly they fly at night, which conceals them even more effectively. Except from bats, who use echo-location instead of vision. Bats consume enormous numbers of moths. But butterflies are colorful, wildly, beautifully colorful. I do not know what good it does them, unless it serves to identify them to other butterflies and help them get sex. Just like the little in-group cliques we find in human high society. The ones we call Social Butterflies. Other than that, bright colors must be deadly dangerous. They attract predators. Many humans, especially children, collect butterflies, and are quite proud of their colorful collections. I am sure you have seen several butterfly collections. Have you ever seen a moth colletion, outside of a museum?

Now add in the random fluttering flight. (By the way, "butterfly" is not a corruption of "flutterby", cute and logical as the urban legend may be. It comes from the Old English word "Buttorfleoge", which literally means "butter fly". Transposing the first letters does not work in Old English.) A bright colored spot that is moving rapidly and unpredictably draws attention more readily than anything except a loud "bang". Remember the first lesson of hiding? "Don't stand up." How, then, do these mindless insects, with their utter disdain of concealment, manage to survive while doing the exact opposite of every other small prey species? How do they avoid being eaten to extinction while blithely shouting "soup's on!" to every bird in eyeshot? Rapid breeding and laying massive quantities of eggs is part of it, but there is also the very same erratic flight pattern that draws attention to themselves.

I love to watch small insectivorous birds swooping upon butterflies. With swift and agile aerobatics, they pursue their prey, striving to get close enough to adroitly snap their beaks on their flying fast food But the flight is unpredictable; how can the bird anticipate a course change when even the butterfly has no idea of what its next move will be? Many times I have seen the swift seeker make a dozen passes while the lucky bug, unconcerned by (and probably unaware of) the attack, manages to blunder into a bush, just out of reach of the frustrated avian. More often the bird succeeds. Never on the first pass; never that I have seen. Usually after four or five fruitless attempts, sometimes landing and launching on a new vector, the bird at last passes closely enough and acts swiftly enough, and flits triumphantly into a tree to devour his prey.

The butterfly is an odd character. It is what it is, it is itself. It does not concern itself with others' opinions, with what anyone else thinks of it. It does as it pleases, flying apparantly for the sole sake of flying, confident it will find food, not worrying about what may happen, not distraught over things that do not affect it. It is floating happiness, and it brings happiness to others. The wildflowers of the forest provide a grace note that enhances the beauty around it; the butterflies are flying flowers. They bring happiness to the flowers by pollinating them, and happiness to the birds by feeding them, and happiness to us by being there.

It is appropriate that, in Indian symbology, the Butterfly represents Eternal Life.

Small Game

I do very little hunting, these days. Mostly in those few states where it is always open season on squirrels, and you do not even need a license to harvest them. Good eating, squirrels. I used to hunt deer, but that was when I had facilities to store the meat. Today, I would have to let most of it go to waste, and I am reluctant to do that, except in a survival situation. I have been told, by many people, that the Indians used to use every part of any bison they killed. It is part of the legend of Lo, the Noble Savage, who never existed. (That is the title of a poem written in the late 1800s bemoaning the cruel oppression of the kindly Red Man; "Lo" means "look" or "behold", but a lotta iggerant folks thought "Lo" was the injun's name. People even more ignorant than the author of the poem.) Sure, they had a use for every part except the bellow, and *could* use every scrap, but they usually did not. In fact, before they got the horse, the favorite technique for hunting bison was to lure a herd to the vicinity of a cliff and panic the beasts into running over the edge. Get fifty or a hundred to slaughter themselves that way, then spend a week preserving the best parts and gathering hides and bones, and leave the larger part of the meat to rot. You can visit the Vore Buffalo Jump in the Black Hills, a small sinkhole which the Indians used for that purpose for hundreds of years. It is yielding a wealth of archaeological treasure. But I do not believe in eating everything I kill. A couple I hunt for pleasure, and leave the carcasses to the scavengers.

Shocking? Not really. Despicable? Not at all! I am talking about mosquitos and flies. I suppose flies are quite nutritious, and perfectly safe to eat if cooked properly, but I have no desire to try them. Instead, they try me, or at least my patience, and I often slaughter them wholesale. It is not that they are dangerous. They are well known to be carriers of disease, but I doubt that is at all common. Sure they *can* carry disease, if they land on an infected corpse, then immediately after walk on a piece of food. But how often does that happen? Usually they walk on cow manure or something similar. Usually they are not fooling around with disease-infested materials. They are *eating* bacteria, not transporting them. And it is not that the flies bite or sting. A few do, but the vast majority are quite harmless. Why kill them?

To understate the case, they are annoying. It is really the only word that accurately applies, but it is so weak. Flies have a remarkable persistence, and an uncanny ability to *return*. You have experienced it: A fly lands on your face. You brush it away, and at buzzes about and returns to exactly the same spot. You wave again, and it flees, then returns again. And again. Five or six times, always returning to within an inch or so of the same place. Why? How? Does it assume this must be an especially fine place, else you would not defend it so? Does it leave behind a chemical marker so it knows where to resume foraging? Did it land there in the first place because it was a particularly rich source of scrummy bacteria? *I* do not know, but they do it.

It is remarkable how well they dodge a swatting hand. They have a circuit linking their eyes and wings. When a threat is approaching and on course to strike them, this circuit triggers the wings, and off flies the fly, quicker than thought. Frogs have a similar circuit. When a fly, or similar sized object, crosses in front of them, the circuit triggers a leap that intercepts the fly in midair. The frog has no control over it. I used to catch frogs that way, with a fishing pole and a bit of bright cloth on the hook. Wave it in front of a frog at the right distance and speed, and the frog will leap and hook itself.

When you are inside a shielded environment, a house or an RV or a tent, you often have a few flies who got in before the room was sealed. Then you have to hunt them down with a flyswatter or, if you do not mind poisoning yourself, bug spray. But outdoors, it is a different story. You cannot kill them all, so why kill any? I have found that, when you are surrounded by a hundred flies, and you kill most of them, then you will remain undisturbed for as much as a half hour. After that, swatting the occasional newcomer is sufficient to keep their presence tolerable. Although it seems they fly in an infinite swarm, there is a limit to their numbers. Usually.

There is a state park, Oasis by name, which is a good place to visit, especially, I am told, for fishing. However, it is located in the heart of the New Mexico dairy country, and it is literally surrounded by dairy farms. By cattle pasturage. By hills of cow manure. It matter not a whit from which direction the wind blows; the odor of manure is always present. There is rich feasting all around for thousands of swarms of squadrons of flies. There is little or nothing that will attract them to the campground, but with so many flies abounding, some will always wander by. Just a few, a very tiny percentage, but a thousandth of a percent of a trillion is still ten million. If you want to hunt flies, I have known no richer ground than Oasis.

I have sat at a picnic table and applied that datum of "wipe out the flies and be undisturbed for a short time". It did not work. Swat one end of the table and kill a few flies, startling the others into flight. Swat the other end and kill a few more, but by this time, they have returned to the first end. It hasn't been two seconds! Sixty strokes to the minute, and in ten minutes you have flattened a thousand flies. Remember the Brave Little Tailor, famed for killing Seven (flies) With One Blow? I have killed thirteen with a single stroke. Maybe more, but that is the most I have counted. It is hopeless. You know you cannot kill them all, but at Oasis, you cannot even dent them. It is a fine place to visit, but do be sure you have a fly-proof refuge. And a flyswatter.

At other places, such as La Posa, the flies are far less numerous, but still enough to annoy. A friend of mine sits by his camp, reading, relaxing, swatting the odd fly He lets the corpses drop to the ground, where the ants gather them and haul them off in a long line to their nest. Sometimes a lizard will spot the largesse, and crouch in the shade, picking off flies as the ants carry them by. Tariff, a toll for crossing his territory The ants do not seem to notice.

Mosquitoes, of course, we swat whenever we can. I do not often need to. When they are too thick, I retreat to my tent, which seals quite nicely with netting over the large windows. Outdoors I wear long-sleeved denim shirts, garters around my ankles, and mosquito netting over my hat. My hands and any exposed skin are nicely coated with bug dope, made of one part pennyroyal oil, two parts castor oil, and three parts pine tar. It has a pleasant smell, washes off easily with soap, leaving the skin soft and moist, and is the most effective product I have tried for keeping the bugs away.

I would be happy to see mosquitoes become extinct. Flies, on the other hand, are only an annoyance to me, and many of my friends, notably lizards, depend on them, so I guess we must tolerate them. We shall still swat them when we can, with good conscience, for there is no possibility of endangering the species.

Good hunting!

Wings

Ravens

As far back as History records, and farther still in lore and legend and myth, Mankind has watched the birds, with envy, admiration, and fear. We have tried to emulate them, to fly with arms transformed into wings, and with the sole and only partial success of hang-gliding, have without exception failed miserably.   We have imbued them with our own feelings and emotions, ascribed to them our own attributes and ideals. Even there, we have failed, utterly. Symbols rarely mean what we say they mean, but that is not surprising. Few people actually say what they mean, or mean what they say.

The Eagle is a magnificent bird, stately, majestic, haughty, with a dignity unmatched in the avian array. He stands erect on the highest prominence available, imperiously surveying his vast domain, ruler of the Wilds, emperor of the air, living symbol of Liberty and Freedom, the epitome of "Don't mess with me!" But it is all symbolism, all apparancy. In actual fact, the eagle is a cowardly, rather stupid carrion-eater that probably tastes like chicken.

The Owl is the symbol of stately wisdom, but it is mostly hot air; eighty percent of its bulk is feathers, the body only a scrawny stick. It hunts by hooting, a peculiarly confusing call that seems to come from all directions at once. It hoots till the prey panics and exposes itself, then silently swoops to an easy meal. If the poor little mouse had simply ignored the owl, it would have remained perfectly safe. The owl should be the symbol of the politician.

The Turkey is a symbol of stupidity. I have seen turkeys carefully look both ways before crossing a road, and I have never seen or even heard of turkey roadkill. Many times I have watched cock turkeys cleverly (and courageously) lure hunters and other people, two-legged and four, away from hens and chicks. Stupid? Benjamin Franklin proposed the wild turkey as the symbol of the nation. Old Ben was no turkey!

The mild, gentle Dove, symbol of peace, is a vicious, ruthless cannibal, when it gets a chance. The symbolism is not totally wrong, as I have known several political doves who matched that description precisely.

And then there is the Raven. Black of feather, beak and claw, black of repute and black of heart. Symbolically, that is. The first bird Noah released was a raven, and it never returned, and is scorned as a result. It probably found some really good carrion and  stayed. Rations on the Ark must have been pretty poor. What did the tigers eat? Unicorns? Then stupid Noah released a dove, which flew back with an olive leaf. If he had had any sense, he would have realized the raven had found land. We know he did, because there were only two ravens in the Ark, and we still have ravens today, so the scout must have survived. Assuming the Flood legend to be accurate.

The raven is smart, probably the most intelligent bird of all. They can learn human speech, which is not surprising if you listen to them in the Wild. Ravens have a huge vocabulary, many sounds that obviously have meaning. They have more words than even coyotes. I know one campground where the ravens tell each other when a newcomer arrives. The Camp Host has learned that phrase, and drives off to greet her new guests whenever she hears it. She maintains that the ravens are alerting her. I do not see why they would unless they simply like her, but it could well be true. She says they have never given her a false alarm. And the ravens not only learn to speak two-leg words ("mimic", their detractors will say), but also to understand them. I once had a raven come calling while I was eating a sandwich; he had surely been tossed scraps of crust by other campers, and hoped I would do the same. Instead, I told him I had tossed some scraps away and pointed to them. He looked where I pointed, cawed, and flapped off to get them. Maybe he understood the words. Maybe he understood the gesture. He clearly understood *something*. The operative word here is "understood". Some have suggested he already knew the scraps were there. If so, why did he not get them first? Camp-Robber jays will do that. It must be some kind of game, but they do steal in preference to accepting gifts. I was once given a large bag of home-grown fruit. I had washed a dozen pears and peaches, and tossed aside a few overripe ones. The local jays went for the discards, but when they figured my attention was elsewhere, they left the discards and tried to get at the ones in the bowl at my side.

Ravens cooperate. Often two will glide in line some thirty feet apart. The one in front calls every few seconds; when it startles a small rodent, the one behind swoops in to make the kill, and they both feed. They will work together to open a bag of bread; one grabs it, waits for the other to get a grip, then both pull in opposite directions.

Ravens are clever. They have learned that plastic grocery bags contain food, and they will open them. It is not the smell of food attracting them. I carry a dozen or more such bags, clean ones, stuffed in one bag. Some ravens once stole it, and carefully removed each bag, checking for food. They will carry off a half-loaf of bread, not opening it till they are safely away. I have watched them open velcro pockets on a knapsack to get at the trail mix. I have even seen them open zippers. Zip-lock bags seem to defeat them, but it is likely that they are not worth opening; the plastic is too easy to tear. They will knock glass jars off of a picnic table to break them, but usually not plastic jars. They will open egg cartons by pecking off the two tabs on the front. They know tinned cans contain food. They have not figured out how to open them (yet), but if you open a can and leave it, a raven might dip in to it, but he also just might fly off with it, if he is strong enough.

Aesop's fables include one about a thirsty raven dropping pebbles into a narrow-mouthed jar to raise the water level high enough to get a drink. It is no fable; I have seen ravens doing exactly that.

The Indians knew all of this, and could see the raven for what it is. Thus in their spirituality, the Raven is beneficent, and is often, like Coyote, associated with the creation of the universe. It is seen as charming and wise, and is looked to for advice and ideas. In Indian symbolism, the Raven is the bearer of magic and light. It is the keeper of secrets, and the message bearer of the Spirits. It is the symbol of Understanding and Knowledge and Transformation. It brings healing to mind and body, and lends clarity to visions.

And with a wry appreciation of the Universe and how it is, they gave the Raven pictograph the meaning of "mischievous trickster". How very appropriate for a Creator Spirit!

Dadratted Doves

We all know the dove. Well, most only know *of* them. Mostly the impressions are legendary or mythological, their reputed characteristics being what we *consider* the dove to have, but bearing little relationship to truth. They are gentle, mild, harmless creatures, and symbolize peace, and hope, and love.

I know the dove. I cannot help it, for they are ubiquitous. Everywhere I go, I find squirrels, and ravens, and . . . doves. When I was a kid, I heard them calling from the woods. I thought it was the voice of owls: "Too-whit-too. Hoo-hoo." That was in New England. In the Rockies, they are more terse. They usually only say "Too-whit-too". But their wings make the same sound everywhere, a clear, high whistling on every downstroke. I wonder at its purpose. Most likely, it is to startle predators.

I often sit silently listening to the world. The deserts are the most quiet; the most common sound is the hyper-chirp of the hummingbird, followed by the extremely varied calls of the coyotes. Insects rarely buzz; aside from the odd fly, they are mostly moths and butterflies. Many small birds of the sparrow and finch types flirt around, but rarely speak. Not the doves, though; after hummingbirds, doves are the most vocal. The forests are much more melodious, and much more varied. Many songbirds chat with each other, singing songs for every occasion. Squirrels chatter and bark, and in the appropriate season, deer and elk and moose will bugle and bellow. Late at night, coyotes howl and javelinas snort, crickets and frogs pour forth their mating calls. Sometimes, rarely, one may hear a puma's eerie moaning wail. Bees supply the buzzing, and mosquitoes whine. And in the right places, at the right times, children and streams chatter and chortle and burble, laughing just because they can. And the doves call, announcing their presence and claiming their territory.

The sounds of running water and running children are joyful and heart-expanding. The cricket choruses are soothing and pacifying. The bugling of bucks is stirring. The singing of birds is sweet and pleasing. The mating calls of doves are just plain flat-out unquestionably annoying. They are worse than the single working-man on Saturday night, than the cowboy at the end of a drive, than the jive cat on any evening. Worse, because those are stereotypes, exaggerations, applicable to only some of each class, and rarely so intense as the sterotype suggests. The mating doves *all* call, *all* the time. They even sound like the stereotypes: "Woo, woo! Woo-hoo!" "Woo, woo! Woo-hoo!" Over and over and over, all day, dawn to dusk, unrelenting, intruding on all else. When such an insistent one perches in a tree less than ten feet from me and blares forth his unmitigated call hour after hour, I entertain serious thoughts of squab for dinner. Where is that slingshot?

Gobblers

The Turkey is a modern symbol of stupidity. This is another sign of the ignorance of the turkeys who simply will not think. Turkeys are smart, sensible, and courageous. Turkeys, like ravens, are the smartest birds I know, but smart in different ways. Ravens are clever-smart; turkeys are wise-smart. I was cruising a divided highway in South Dakota and saw, far ahead, a wild turkey dart across my side and over the divider. He stopped at the edge and looked. He waited, watching as a couple of cars swept by, waited till there was a long gap before the next car, then darted across. Stop, look, and listen. That is when I realized I had never seen or even heard of a turkey roadkill. Just yesterday, though, I almost saw my first turkey roadkill. In fact, I almost killed it myself.

I do not often see turkeys in the woods. Usually it is on or by a road, and almost always a lone tom. At least, I only *see* the tom. I was cruising into town, doing the limit in a forty-five zone, when I saw ahead of me a turkey family crossing the road. In front was Mama, leading eight or nine half-grown chicks (this being early August), with Papa bringing up the rear and chivvying the youngsters along. He saw me and stopped. She saw me, too, and quickened her pace, and the little ones followed her lead. I, of course, was braking as hard as I needed to to stop before reaching the flock. They were actually never in any danger, but naturally they could not be sure of it, and would be fools, not turkeys, to count on it. Old Tom just stood there in the left half of my lane, drawing my attention and just daring me to hit him. Holding my attention, at the likely risk of his own life, while his family scurried to safety. I stopped about six feet from him, and he nodded at me (or possibly just bobbed his head), and calmly crossed the road. I had pulled to the side, so I dismounted and unlimbered my camera. I had to wait for a dozen or two motorcycles to pass (this was forty miles west of Sturgis, a few days before the commencement of the Rally), then crossed the road to try for some good shots.

Stupid? Not a chance! Smart, sensible, and courageous. Call me a turkey, and I will take it as a compliment. Benjamin Franklin proposed the wild turkey as the symbol of the nation. Old Ben was no turkey!

So here I am, sitting by my tent, minding my own business, enjoying the quiet sounds of the forest, the slight whisper of the gentle breeze in the pines, the buzz of the occasional bee, the chirp of the robin, the croak of the raven, when a sharp raucous racket bounces out of the South. It can only be described as a gobble, and only because that is the name we have given to the sound. "Gubble" would be better. "Gubbleubbleubbleubble" is even closer. It is the mating call of the wild turkey. Have you ever seen the old movie "Sergeant York"? Gary Cooper plays the hero. There is a turkey-shoot scene, in which he imitates the turkey's gobble, and he gets it just right. See the movie, hear the gobble, and you will recognize it in the wild. And I recognize it now, many calls, many birds.

I take my camera, and creep around the underbrush quietly, heading for the area to which the turkeys seem to be converging. If I am lucky, and cautious, and lucky, and very quiet, and especially if I am lucky, I may spot a few birds in the brush and get a picture or two. I have several pictures of turkeys on and near roads, mostly moseying, but I have yet to get a good shot of one in the woods. I pick a spot with a good open view in several directions, make myself comfortable, and wait. All I need now is patience, and a compliant turkey.

Spring lies across the mountains, and there are a lot of wild turkeys under the Mogollen Rim. They are protected at this time of year, and smart enough to know it. Turkeys are very hard to find during the hunting season, but will almost walk right up to a two-legs the rest of the time. They are a little wary, but not much. Ten, maybe fifteen feet, is considered by them to be a safe distance. Today the woods are teeming with them. Their calls come from the South, and are soon answered from East and West and North, and every point between. The cocks are after the hens. They want their wimmin, they want to make turkey-chicks. Gobbles abound and resound, and with just a bit of real *listening*, soon become discrete, individual, unique as human voices. One of them, probably the biggest, since the pitch is slightly lower than the others, moves slowly toward the West. Other voices move away from him. If he is bigger than the others, one would suspect he can outfight them, and thus would secure the wimmin for himself. Yes, plural. The turkey is polygynous. I have often seen one cock turkey shepherding a small harem of hens, at least three or four, possibly more, but they can be very discreet and difficult to see. Many are the times a turkey has revealed himself to me, intentionally attracting my attention, then moseying along slowly, as if inviting me to follow. And he *is* inviting me. If I turn my back on him and search in the other direction, I will as likely as not find his wives, the flock away from which he is trying to divert me. Oh, yes, they are smart. But I am smarter. I think I am. This is just like hunting, it *is* hunting, but instead of shooting with a rifle, I shoot with a camera. And yes, when I hunt turkey, I use a rifle, not a shotgun. A wild turkey is an awfully big target, and if I can see one, I can hit it with a bullet. It is the seeing that is the hard part. I try a couple of gobbles, to no affect; I am not as good at it as Gary. I shut up, and wait. Patience pays off most of the time.

Patience is easy. I would not be upset if I saw no turkeys today, because the woods are so beautiful, just in themselves. The air is cool, the trees stand silently, not visibly moving at all. Robins sing. Woodpeckers hammer. Squirrels scamper through the duff, and up and down the trunks. The air is clear and clean, sweet and fresh. That is especially good, because one thing I cannot do now is have a cigarette. Well, I could, but won't. Fire danger is extreme, and even with the greatest care, a spark could possibly escape me. No, I shall be patient, and wait till I get back to camp. Patience is easy. Patiently waiting for a turkey to amble by.

I hear the gobbles on either side. They do not sound too far off. Careful peering yields no sightings. I cannot use binoculars; too much body motion. The little prey animals know that any motion is many times more visible than total stillness. I sit as still as I can, striving to move only my eyeballs. This works wonderfully well for deer. There is one coming by now. Rather stupid things, these deer. They cannot recognize a two-legs that is not moving. I have often used that knowledge in stalking deer. You just hold yourself very still, utterly motionless, until the deer lowers his head to feed. Then you take two or three steps, carefully placing your feet where they will make no sound, and cautiously not brushing against anything that might make a noise, then freezing before the deer raises his head. Often the deer will twitch his tail just before looking up, but not always. If you stalk a twitcher, you can profit by this, but it is more sure to simply be patient. When the deer does look around again, he will not see you, if you do not move. Actually, he will *see* you, may even stare at you for many seconds (and Oh! How long those seconds can feel!), but if you hold perfectly still, he will apparantly decide you are nothing more than an old tree trunk, and go back to feeding. Then you take a couple more steps and freeze for his next perusal. He will see you again, every time he scans for danger, but if you do not move, you must be a tree. He never seems to realize that this old dead stump is closer every time he looks. It is not visibly moving *now*, so it must not be dangerous. I have worked my way up to within a few yards of a deer, and he suspected nothing till I snapped a picture. I only get the one photo. By the time I can work the shutter a second time, the deer is generally out of sight, over the hills and far away, thoroughly panicked by a two-legs who managed to magically appear out of nothing.

This deer wanders along, complacently browsing, content in the knowledge that there is no danger in sight. She casually crosses the small meadow, and drifts away over the ridge, never suspecting she had been under constant observation. I took no pictures of her, for fear the sound and small motion might spook her, and thus alert my real prey, the turkeys. The turkeys are not fooled by motionlessness. They know that things can hold still, that two-legs *will* hold still, and they will watch for shapes, not just movements. Stillness does not make one invisible, it only does not draw attention. Off in the distance, I spot a turkey. Spot him by his motion. I do not move. I will wait till he is much closer before attempting to use my camera. But he comes no closer; he spots me, perhaps by shape, probably by color. Very little in the woods is the color of blue denim. I need a gillie suit for a decent chance.

I still hear the crowd calling, gobbling from many various directions, but they seem to be drawing off towards the West. I continue to wait, while squirrels scamper and sparrows flit. The gobbles now come only from the West; apparently I chose the wrong spot for my hide. No matter. I will try again tomorrow, but better prepared. I will wear brown, and bring a brown tarp to hide behind. In fact, I will set it up this afternoon. Who knows, it might work. Then again, I usually failed in a turkey hunt. Still, it is worth a try.

When I stand up, several squirrels and a dozen birds dash off in utter panic.

Hummers

Not the modern multi-use military vehicles. Not the tinfoil imitations popped out by Detroit. I mean the bird, the most amazing, most admirable flyer, the sky-otter, the aspen of the air. The Hummingbird.

The hummingbird is the master of flight in all forms It is the only bird that can hover for more than a few seconds. Some birds, raptors and scavengers, often appear to hover, but while they are stationary relative to the ground, they are still flying, moving through the air, balanced on an updraft, or soaring into the wind at the same speed at which the wind is blowing. The hummingbird hovers, like a helicopter, fanning his wings in a precise pattern, holding his position exactly where he wants to be. I have watched one leave his treetop and rise vertically a hundred, maybe two hundred feet, straight up, then back down, repeatedly, slowly or swiftly, but always straight. They will hover by a flower, delicately sipping the nectar, then zip, almost instantaneously, to another blossom a foot or two away. Their wings move so fast they are only a blur, and their passage through the air makes a constant buzz. I have heard the wing flaps of larger birds, ravens and eagles and vultures, whoosh once or twice each second; the hummingbird makes a hundred strokes per second. Even with a fast shutter speed, a camera usually records only a blur. Their metabolism when flying is astonishingly fast. Their hearts beat over twelve hundred times per second, and when they land, can drop to a mere hundred eighty, or even fifty when sleeping. I once held a hummingbird in my hand. He had flown into a window and knocked himself senseless. I picked him up, and he lay unconscious, not even twitching, for five or six seconds. Then, in an instant, so quickly I could discern no transition, he was in full flight, and gone.

Most people believe the hummingbird lives solely on the nectar of flowers, but that is actually only a small part of their diet, and mostly used for flying. Aviation fuel. They also consume bugs, tiny insects and spiders. I have often seen one hover in the midst of a dense swirling cloud of midges, his tongue flicking like a miniature lightning bolt, scarfing the insects right out of the air. And of course, there are always the

hummingbird feeders, bottles of sugar water with bright red nozzles, pantomime flowers, to access the artificial nectar. Hummingbirds are strongly attracted to bright red, perhaps naturally, but possibly because they have learned that we two-legs always make feeders red. They certainly know about feeders, and understand them, and are aware that we control them. When I lay out my gear at a new campsite, invariably the hummingbirds will come to check it out. They zip among the bags and bottles, investigating every spot of red. They even fly into my tent, especially when I am sitting inside. They hover in front of me and demand "Where is the feeder?" For a long time I did not carry one. Now I do. When I dwelt in a city, I usually maintained a feeder. Many times I would be sitting in the yard and a hummingbird would fly over and hover a foot in front of my face. When he saw he had my attention, he would flit over to the feeder and come back, pause, and repeat, over and over, till I stood up and checked it. Invariably, it would be empty. I would humbly apologize and thank the little fellow for bringing it to my attention, then wash and fill the bottle. When I hung it back up, the bird would hover by me for a few seconds before returning to the feeder. Clearly, he knew that I filled his feeder, and thanked me for it.

Some hummingbirds wear subdued shades of brown and black, but most, especially the males, have green and blue and red feathers. When they catch the light at just the right angle, they glow with a shimmering metallic glisten. If such a bright hummingbird was as large as a peacock, it would take the blue ribbon in any avian beauty pageant.

Hummingbirds are usually very territorial. I once had a yard that was at or near the junction of at least three territories. There was one pair who clearly held my feeder to be their own private property, and staunchly defended it against any and all trespassers. The female would spy an intruder and dash off to find her mate, who would come arrowing in to the attack. Usually the invader would retreat at once, but sometimes, especially when there was a female present, the two males would flutter in mid-air, battering with their wings till one had had enough. The loser would depart, closely followed by the victor. And then a third pair, who had been quietly observing from a nearby bush, would swoop in and guzzle nectar till the indignant victor returned, then flash away, laughing at their clever strategy. But in some areas, the residents are more gregarious, or at least more tolerant. Often there will be four or five feeding at the same time. Once I saw a large feeder being patronized by over a dozen (it was impossible to count them, for they moved so fast). There was a bit of bickering, and a few aerial tussles, but by and large, they put up with each other's presence.

The voice of the hummingbird is another source of sheer astonishment. There is a sharp click, like the sound you might make clicking your tongue. The bird may give one click, or a short series, or rattle them off like running your finger along the tip of a comb's teeth, and sounding much the same. The most astounding is the chirp used as a declaration of territory, or as a mating call. The male takes a deep breath, squeezes every muscle, and emits a sharp note nineteen times his size. When I first heard this call, I looked around, searching for the bird that made it, but there were none present except a tiny hummingbird. After long observation, I finally saw one in the act of calling. I had to see it several times before I could accept that such a miniscule throat could produce such a large sound. Truth is so often stranger and less believable than fiction. And that brings us to the third sound, a sweet and gentle peep, a chirp, a chime, really, for it sounds exactly like a tiny bell, a *tink*. Usually it is a single note, but sometimes they are strung together, a tinkle of seven or ten tinks per second, a trill, a jingle, the voice of the fairy. I can just see a besotted proto-Irishman, two or three thousand years ago, lying in a drunken haze in a rich green meadow. He awakens to blearily see an iridescent red and green hummingbird investigating his red nose, and hears the laughing bells. The vision vanishes in a seeming flash of light, and the befuddled man sits up and cries, "Shure and be(hic)gorrah! 'Tis the little people, the fairy folk!"

And you thought fairies were mythical!

The Forest in the Stream

Fish love the trees. The dead trees. The trunks and branches that have fallen into the water form dams and pools and eddies and falls. Mosses and algae grow on them, and bacteria that feed on the decomposing wood. Insects and larvae, tadpoles and minnows, all swarm to feed, and the fish feast upon them. Chez Bois, the five-star restaurant of the woods. Much better than sterile rocks. Granted, the wooden dams do not last long. In two years, or three, the barrier will rot and dissolve, or float elsewhere in the next spring rise. The restaurant business is always chancy, and redecoration is frequent. But what is time to a fish? The future does not exist, not yet. And when it does, it will be Now, not the Future. That is all the fish knows, the eternal Now. And Now is time to eat. The fish lazes in a small eddy, waiting for something tasty to drift by. He flicks slowly to a log and samples a bit of salad, maybe a tadpole or two. A luckless fly drops over a branch and down the trout's throat. It is in many ways much like the forest through which it flows.

How boring the stream would be without the logs and the boulders, the rocks and pebbles, meanders and falls! Straight sides, steady drop, no ripples or rapids, pools or pits, overhangs or undertows. No more than a canal. No place to rest in the steady current, no falls to replenish the oxygen, no deep pools or dark hollows to hide in when predators stalk. It would be more like a city park with its paved walks and "Keep Off The (mowed) Grass" rules and strategically sited trees. But this is wild, this is more like the true forest. More, even, than you think. Does it not contain trees? And branches? And birds?

    "Birds", did I say? Yes. Not wading along the shore. Not sitting on top. Not even doing a quick dive for a fish. There are little birds walking along the bottom, seeking out morsels and delicacies. Honest, there are!

It is a little bird, only four or five inches long, and drab, a pale gray-brown, and does not appear to be distinguished or unusual in any way that is normally visible. Normally. It is shy, and very likely to fly away at the first sign of any two-legs. It is not at all common, in my experience, for I have only rarely seen it, and even more rarely been able to photograph it. But today I (finally) got lucky, and caught it in action.

Appearances not withstanding, the Dipper (as the Water Ouzel is more properly named, in America) is actually a most distinguished, even unique, bird, for it feeds underwater. Yes, there are several birds that will dive into the water after fish. Some slice through the surface in a power dive and nab a fish that had been seen from far above. Some will do a surface dive and nibble at weeds and other edible on the bottom. The penguin actually swims, literally flying underwater, in pursuit of fish. The Dipper, however, lands on a rock in a swiftly flowing stream, and studies the waters around it. Flitting from

rock to rock, it selects a suitable spot, and wades into the water. When the depth is to its liking, it gives a flirt of its tail, and disappears beneath the surface. Then it does not swim; it *walks* along the bottom, probably gripping gravel in its tiny claws, rooting and pecking among pebbles exactly as a robin does on dry land, snapping up insects and larvae and whatever else that it finds. Shortly, it hops out onto a rock and stands, perfectly dry, getting its breath for another foray. It is not a diving bird. Diving birds swim through the water, only touching the bottom with their bills. The ouzel does not swim. It walks. It climbs and clambers among the stones, then walks out of the water, and only then does it fly. At least, I have never seen one do otherwise.

When I first wrote of the Forest in the Stream, noting the parallels between waters and woods, little did I dream that the woods in the waters held literal birds Now I am watching the trees. Are there any fish in them?

Roots

Green

Green. A short word, a simple word, yet it carries so much meaning. Green. Which color is green? There are so many, every hue between yellow and blue. We have yellow and beige and dandelion and umber and all of the names of tans and browns, which are more or less dark yellows. We have blue and turquoise and aqua and azure and cyan and many many more names of blues. We have red and crimson and scarlet, bright and fiery. But we only have green, and sea-green and pea-green and grass-green and so on. The painter may have special names for special shades, but common terms? It seems they are all green. They are this-green and that-green, but always something-green. And there are so many forms, such a plethora of varieties. The Irish claim forty shades, and that is only on one island. I sit in the forest and count the greens around me, only the distinct and undeniably different shades. I stop at twenty, though there are many more. And this is a high-altitude Ponderosa forest. What would we find in the primeval forests of Siberia and Canada, or in the lush rain forests of Western Oregon?

We love green. We treasure green. The sailor loves the blue of the sea, but looks always for the green of the land. The rancher, the cowboy, the wanderer of the West, loves the tans and browns of the plains, but searches out the green that means water and coolth and rest. Even the dwellers in the stone cities seek out green and cultivate it in lawns and parks and tree-lined boulevards. We crave green and will not live without it, for we know we can not live without it. Even those greens that are not of life are precious. In spite of the artificial value of the common diamond, maintained by marketing and restriction of supply, it is the green emerald that commands the highest price and the true place of honor.

Green is synonymous with good, with growth, with youth, with richness, with life itself. Green is freshness, coolness, exuberance, newness. It is also jealousy, envy, queasiness and sickness. It means newly-formed and unripe and ripe and spoiled. It means everything. What other color is so rich with meaning? White is pure and clean, and fear and death. Black is foulness and evil, and profit. Red is heat and rage, yellow is fear and sickness and warmth, blue is sadness and loss, peace and serenity, orange is . . . orange.

And green is contradiction: Plants are green because they reject the green light. Red, orange, yellow, blue, these are absorbed and used to build sugars, food for the plants, and for beasts and birds and bugs. All of the green light is reflected, rejected, and thus becomes the symbol of life. But that is the way the universe works, fooling us into believing the opposite of what is, weaving a mystery around everything, for if we fully perceived the Truth, all would vanish into the nothingness from which it was formed.

There is so much we do not know, so much we do not perceive. Green is green, and it means what we say it means, but only because we say so. Green is not cool, except it is because we say it is, nor is it fresh or foul or young or aged or inherently good. But it is all of this and more, and it is only because that is what it means to us, because green is Life and we are Life, and we say so. And today, here in the hills, all is beautiful, blue and brown and yellow, and green, green, green. Because I say so.

The Philosophy of Trees

The word Philosophy is from the Greek, and means Love of Knowing. A philosophy is a set of rules or guidelines by which one lives, or should live, or wants to live. It is a description or a statement of what the world or life is, or should be, or one wants it to be. It is not a fixed and immutable thing; it changes and grows as one's knowledge and perception and experiences grow. It is not the exclusive domain of ancient erudite German academics. It is not rarified, abstruse, esoteric, difficult, and hard to understand. It is easy, very easy. In truth, everyone and everything is a philosopher and has a philosophy, and the simpler a philosophy is, the more likely it is to be valid, true, a worthwhile and above all *usable* tool. Because that is all that philosophy is: a tool to enhance living, a tool to help one to survive better.

Trees have philosophies. You can read them by just looking at the trees, at what they do. Their activities, their purposes are to absorb sunlight in order to grow, to survive as long as possible, and to scatter many seeds. A typical spruce, the kind most used for Christmas trees, grows straight and true, up as fast as it can, while sending out branches as straight and as far as it can. It takes on a perfect conical shape. It has a simple philosophy, the simplest possible: To spread its needles as far as it can to gather as much sunlight as it can. In the far North, the tree adds "and slope branches downward so the snow will fall off and not break branches".

Other conifers, notably the Ponderosa Pine, have a more aggressive philosophy: Reach for the sky. Get as tall as you can and spread branches above everyone else. Then jettison the lower branches, the ones now in shade that cannot capture much sunlight. And while you are doing this, grow a really thick bark. You see, these trees live in areas that are subject to frequent fires which race through at ground level. The thick bark is armor that normally shields the vital inner bark from the heat of the fire, and the absence of lower branches denies the flames a path to the growing upper tree. The saplings and smaller trees are often killed, but a mature tree of a century or more is immune to most fires.

Many deciduous trees such as the oak and the chestnut use a completely different philosophy: Height is good, but spread is dominant. Grow thick, strong branches that extend horizontally as far as possible. Harvest sunlight across the widest area, shading the ground below to discourage anything else from rising high enough to block the sun.

The aspen philosophy has more - - - well, *panache*. The aspen is different from what we usually envision as a tree. It is more of a root, or a root system, that sends up trunks over a widely dispersed area, in at least one case, well over a hundred acres. It does not thrive in shade; it needs plenty of direct sunlight. It has thin bark and is not resistive to fire at all, and yet its philosophy is based on fire. The mature firs and pines are immune to most fires, but inevitably, though rarely, perhaps hundreds of years apart, there comes a wildfire so great, so intense, that it kills even the biggest trees. It kills everything. At least, everything above the ground. Then the next shoot sent up from the aspen roots reports back "All clear!" The shade is gone. More and more shoots rise, and in three or five years,the ashen wasteland has become a solid thicket of aspen saplings. This is the aspen philosophy: When the pines are away, the aspens will play. Tens of thousands of saplings leap up and exuberantly grow. At ten feet they thin out the lesser trunks, at twenty they form a glade one can easily stroll through, at thirty they are a true forest in their own right. And all of this time, the frolicing leaves are pouring nutrients into the massive root system, a warehouse, a larder to live on over the long decades and centuries of waiting, waiting, till, as sure as sunrise, the blanketing forest falls again. For even as the older aspens are dancing in the wind, new pines are sprouting in the shade below. They will grow through the shorter aspen, rise to their rightful heights, and shade out the frivolous forest which had sheltered their birth. And the aspen will settle down once more, and wait, dreaming of the next Festival of Fire.

We call the palms trees, but they are not. They are more closely related to grasses. Thus it is not surprising that they have a simpler philosophy than the true trees, for they are a simple folk, and not very bright. It simply grows new fronds from its peak, one after another, over and over, to spread in the sun, bend flat under the pressure of the next new frond, flop over, droop, die, and fall away. The palm's sole objective is to reach up, up, up, raise its fronds and wave them high, gushing into the sky, a solid fountain of leaves. But its roots are weak, tiny tendrils that eventually fail under the increasing stress of the wind using the trunk as an ever-extending lever. The palm falls, but if any roots remain in the ground, the single-minded simpleton will carry on, bending its bole at the right angle to continue up, up, up, raising its fronds and waving them as always, as all it can do. Simple, crude, but it works. There is no denying the fact. It does work.

As all of these philosophies work. Different, even contradictory, but they work. Those that do not work die out with their philosophers. For that is the purpose of philosophy: To enable one to survive, to not die out. There have been many religions and so-called philosophies that forbade procreation. There are even some in existence today. But no existing one is older than a generation or so. They cannot be. Their goal is, quite literally, to die out, to die, to become extinct. And they succeed right well. To be philosophic is to live. The cult of Zero Population Growth is such a pseudo-philosophy. It preaches "Stop growing". Stupid. Foolish. Nature knows. Every species alive today knows. Grow! Expand! Flourish! Even the mountains know this. I can hear the Appalachians telling the Rockies "In a few million years, you will be brought low, as we have". The San Gabriel Mountains still grow; I watched them rise a foot in one earthquake. They know.

I care nothing for the dire warnings of crushing catastrophe. I look at the facts, at the records of history. That which does not grow, shrinks and dies. Yes, expansion and growth will surely bring problems. But stagnation and decline will certainly, unavoidably, bring extinction.

The trees know.

Polluted Forest

Pollute: (verb) To make a thing unfit for the use for which it was intended

I have only rarely seen a pristine, natural forest, save in old photographs. *Very* old photographs. With a few exceptions, they are not jungles, not disorderly ramparts of tangled dead branches and thick-set brush, not closely packed masses of saplings jostling their ancient ancestors. Most of them are more like parks, with open, airy expanses in the shade of vigorous young trees and mature and well-spaced monarchs.

We have been polluting and ruining our forests for over a hundred years, all with the best intentions. We thought that we were protecting and preserving them. We did not do much; we just put out the fires. All of them. All of the dead branches and leaves accumulated. The saplings survived and grew to form flammable ladders linking the ground to the crowns. And then when fire came, instead of sweeping the forest clear of the waste, it became a fierce furnace that swept the forest away. What should have been a broom became a bulldozer. Then we perceived our error, and changed our ways, but still, we must pay for it. Now we have to clean up the mess ourselves. We must cut down the excess young trees, chop away the crowded brush, haul away the dense piles of dead wood, and do many prescribed burns, small fires we can control, to simulate the naturally-occuring fires. A Forest Service Fire Specialist once told me that it costs just as much, if not more, acre for acre, to clean up and restore a forest as it does to fight a wildfire. And we are paying that price, slowly, while still fighting many of the big conflagrations that wipe out areas which we have not yet cleaned up.

We are doing better, much better, but still do not have it quite right. We still fight too many fires. I just saw a Forest Service brochure about forest fires. It described prescribed fires, burning when and where we decide, and wildfires, started by lightning or foolishness, *not* by plan. It said only prescribed fires are good, and wildfires are never good. Still a bit on the arrogant side, fellows.

Here is a better plan. Not perfect, I am sure, but perfection is pretty hard (or impossible) to attain, and not really necessary.

Prevent foolish fires. Continue to educate people on how and when to handle campfires, on the safe way to smoke, or not smoke, or use fireworks, and so on, in forests and grasslands. Ban any fires when forest conditions warrant. Allow campfires and smoking and fireworks when conditions allow. That is good, and we pretty much do it now. Good job. But do not take it too far. I know a forest where smoking is prohibited. Period. Any time. Torrential downpours that have been falling all week? No matter. No smoking. This is foolish, even stupid.

Some fires we must fight. The ones that threaten homes and businesses must be contained and put out, but only where they actually threaten. Protect the buildings, but let the rest of the area burn. Lightning strikes in a wilderness and starts a wildfire or two? *Let it burn!* It is natural, it *works*. It does not destroy the forest, it clears away the old and makes room for the new. The forest grows back. Even when every tree over thousands of acres is destroyed, the forest still grows back. Yellowstone burned in 1988, and people bemoaned the utter destruction, that the forest would not recover for a hundred years. Take a look now. It *has* recovered. After just a couple of decades, in most areas the only way you can tell there was a fire is by the still-standing snags, and even they will be gone soon. The forest knows what it is doing, it is expert at handling fire. It knows better than we do. Leave it alone. Don't mess with it. Let it burn. And, incidentally, save all of that money being burned up in fire suppression, and human lives.

Unfortunately, given the mess we have created, we cannot implement this all at once. Stop fighting *any* fires, and we could lose half of our forests or more within a decade. We will have to stretch it out over a century or more. Let about one or two percent burn each year, and spread it out fairly uniformly. Do not allow an entire forest to burn at once. No, limit it to a few percent of each forest. More or less. Strive to keep plenty of mature forest, but slowly get every acre either cleaned up by prescribed burn, or restarted by nature. Then, when a section has been restored, *leave it alone!* Mother Nature can handle it. She has a plan that has worked for millions of years.

In this case, Mother knows best.

The Corpse

I found a body in the woods, the remains of an old, old man. He had lived there long ago, and for a very long time. He was once a tree, a juniper, of the type called "alligator". He had lived for hundreds of years, four hundred, five hundred. Who can say? But he was not immortal. Eventually, his time was told, and his spirit passed on. Perhaps it inhabits another tree, or a squirrel, or a bird. I do not know. All that I know is what he left behind, as a monument to his life.

Theses junipers grow slowly, for this is a harsh land, dry. During times such as today, one may well wonder that any life can survive here at all. There is now no moisture in the soil, none, or if there is, it lies very deep. Ah, but more will come. There are days when ample water flows freely. Though it is not here now, it has left its signs, marks on the ground, deep gullies in the hills.

That is the nature of this land, today. Signs and portents, marks and indicators, history written in the rocks and soil, tales of what was, engraved in the trees.

The old man was lucky, and thus survived to grow strong. And once he had survived so far, he continued, growing stronger every year, until he was probably the strongest and stoutest tree for a long, long way. His trunk was thick, and his main branches, too. Why, his branches are thicker than most of the trees that surround his monument. And from the main branches, smaller ones extend, ending in profusions of twigs.

What a marvelous climbing tree he must have been! I would have loved him. I would have spent hours working my way up, and down, and out in all directions. And if I had fallen, there would have been more branches to catch me, to slow my fall, to deposit me in the deep duff that still surrounds him today. Now, though, the duff is dry, crackling dry, powder dry. It will be restored in a couple of months, when the monsoon comes, when the soil again becomes moist, for a while.

Much of his bark is gone, but not in the powder-based chunks that are usual on the ancient dead pines. No, there are no loosening slabs to crack and calve like icebergs, dropping sections as their grips grow weaker than their weight. In fact, it appears that the tree has lost little bark since it died, years, decades ago. Decades. Perhaps a hundred years, the monument has withstood the slow decay of time, for just as these trees require many years to transform from what we would call a sapling, so do their bones persist long, long after they have abandoned growth. The branches are thick with lichen, the slow-growing amalgam of fungus and algae that thrives upon bare rock. Long and wide bare patches expose the wood of the trunk, but the borders of the bark are not rough, broken scars, but bear gentle, rolled edges. Clearly, there was a wound; perhaps lightning, perhaps a falling neighbor, gashed the living body, scraped or seared the living bark, and the tree patiently repaired the edges, sealing in the sap that circulates from rootlet to leaf-tip. Such wounds and scars are common on alligator juniper. A branch in the midst of the scar was sheared off, leaving the curious whorl of a knot, a blemish, a feature, a footnote in the tale of a tree. But there are many such scars on this ancient warrior, battle-scars of a bitterly fought war, a war for the survival of his kind. Did he win the war? Yes, he surely must have, for his kinfolk, his descendants, stand thickly around, dominating the land for many miles.

And yet, there are few near by. The old man is crowded by young growth, ponderosa pines to whom he may have given their start, shaded and protected beneath his overstretched branches, guarded from too-intense heat and tearing hail, growing till they were strong enough to be supported by their own roots. Then the old man died, and his young charges emerged from his shadow, now overtopping him, and mingling their fresh green branches with his gnarled and bare ones. His corpse will likely disintegrate where it stands, dropping piece by piece and particle by particle to the forest floor, but if its base should give way, should the solid mass topple as a single piece, it would surely take several of his companions down with him. Dead and decaying as it is, the trunk is still strong, massive, sound. How deeply do the roots run? How thick is this soil, how far to the bedrock? Are those roots locked inside crevices and cracks? If so, they will never loose their holds till they have decayed to dust.

Here in the forests, life is very short for most of the living things. Weeks or months for insects, a handful of years for small birds and mammals, less than a score for most everything else. Only for the trees, the lucky ones, the happy few who survive to maturity, can life be measured in centuries, and for them, well, there is no telling what their upper limit may be; I know one tree who claims over eighty thousand years, and I believe him. And even when life has departed, there is no brief passing, no quick gulp and swallow, no decay for a few weeks, to return the remains to the soil. Such is the fate of the many. The few, the giants, the collossi, do not pass so easily. They required centuries to achieve their dominant standing; they will insist on decades to finally vanish forever. And while they are gradually diminishing, we can read their tales, remember their adventures, and dream of their golden days. Then we can look around, at the ones that still live, the ones that struggle as these passed titans once struggled, and see, if we look, the same adventures unfolding anew. If we look.

Dancing Aspen

Most of what people believe and do and say is based on their own prejudices and considerations. It is rarely reasoned, except insofar as they align it or justify it by their own beliefs. The fact is, most people will do almost anything to avoid having to think.

The Aspen is called the Quaking Aspen; quaking, meaning quivering, trembling, probably because of the way the leaves flutter in the wind. Somebody labelled them, and everyone else accepted the label, probably without ever seeing the trees. But it is not at all accurate. To see this, all you have to do is *look*. The leaves do not quake or tremble; that would be a sort of vibration, with connotations of fear or timidity. The leaves twist and turn, skitter and shimmer, flutter and frolic, as if the wind was tickling and tittilating them. They *dance* in the air! True, the trunks do not move, but what of it? They do not waltz, they hand-jive. They aspens are playing with the wind.

The aspen are a playful, frolicsome, irrepressible breed. This is obvious from their lifestyle. They sport in the wake of disaster, swiftly repopulating acres devastated by wildfire. They quickly form fast-growing groves and forests, enriching the stripped soil with dropped leaves and providing a protected environment for the pines, the next phase of the forest cycle. The pines grow to overtop the aspens and tower above them, shading them out and establishing the mature forest of stately grandfathers. Then the aspen retreat, draw back into the ground. They do not fight back or revolt. They know the cycle, they know what will come. They withdraw, and rest.

The leaves are lost, the branches drop, the trunks fall, but the roots remain, surviving on stored sunlight. Occasionally a shoot is sent up as a scout, a short-lived sapling that reports back a small amount of new nutrients, the paucity revealing to the roots that the forest still stands. But the roots are patient. They lie quiescent, biding their time, waiting until one day, without fail, the Fire returns and the forest falls. All is black and dead, as far as can be seen, ashes and charcoal, ruined monarchs, standing or fallen, dead remnants in an utterly dead ruin. But the life awaits, unseen. Roots remain, underground, safely stashed where the fire can never reach. The scout raises his head, looks around. There is nothing but light. He drinks it in, sending plentiful sustenance back to the roots. They react, sending more shoots, and more, and more. In a forest instant a new grove has appeared, the gray becomes green, the fauna return, and the cycle repeats.

Small wonder the aspens dance; they *live* to dance. After years of patiently waiting, they leap into the light and make the most of it while they can, an Aspen Saturday Night. Soon the stolid pines will push aside the pioneers and build the forest city. But there are always *some* frontiers, and sometimes, when conditions are right, a frontier will persist. In Utah there is an aspen grove of over a hundred acres, but only one tree. There are thousands, tens of thousands of trunks, but only one root system. Every trunk is a part of the organism, the largest single living thing on the planet. Perhaps the oldest as well, for though each trunk is young, no one can say when the first trunk, long gone back to the soil, sprouted from a seed. Of all living things, it has grown the most, lived the most, and, surely, had the most fun.

I would rather be an aspen than any other tree.

Old Grandfather Live Oak

There is a piquant beauty in the bones of old oaks and their kin. Their burls and whorls and twists and gnarls speak silently of storms and snows, of lost limbs and lightning strikes, of bold invasions by insect borers and wounds from wildfire. They speak of decades of struggle to survive, of infinitely patient perseverance, of eventual victory even in death. Even in death he stands, stubborn, stripped of leaves and limbs and bark, dead roots still embedded in the stony soil, still tenaciously grasping the bedrock, still gripping cracks and crevices he opened in his youthful vigor and then widened in his mature determination to obstinately stand against all odds. Still stands as he slowly returns to the soil he helped build, still a part of the great world of Life.

One thinks of the mighty oak that defies the storm, that holds strong against its strongest blast, till at last its strength is not enough, the soil itself betrays the roots, and the defiant giant falls in defeat. Not so for our ancient grandfather. He never fell, even in death, and he never shall fall, for his roots are locked in the very bones of the land, not in the soft flesh of the soil. When his bare bones eventually crumble, they will no longer be wood, but a soft punk, the stored energies long ago eaten by insect and moss.

I came upon him on a forested ridge in the high vales at the base of the Mogollen Rim, leaning on the shoulder of a young pine. We sat together for a while, me running my fingers over the grey fibers, reading his memories written in wood, he speaking through them of his long and leisurely life in the wild woods. He spoke of the first men he had seen, hunters stalking the elk, of arrogant bears and chittering long-eared squirrels, of robins and jays and black ravens, all seeking his fruits, and of coyotes seeking the squirrels. He spoke of many branches lost to winds, to struggles among animals, to insects and diseases barely defeated. He spoke of the storm that shattered his trunk, but left him a strong branch which became his new trunk. He spoke of the lightning that left a long gash in his bark, a death wound through which the last disease finally crept to his heart. He spoke quietly, with satisfaction, for he had lived long, had fed many a hungry beast, and left behind him a legacy of new fertile soil, and his descendants still lived. He was content.

I left him, then, thanking him for being there. I left him with a wish that I could have seen him in his prime.

There is magic in the world. Some say it is no more than coincidence, some say it is fantasy and wishful thinking. They may well be right, but it is still true. The trees have power. They gather the light of the sun, and store it in forms that other life can use. They break the rocks and build rich soil from their dropped leaves and discarded bark. They drop seeds and nuts; the birds and the beasts eat most of them, but also carry some off to sprout and grow into a new generation of trees. They do build their own world, and change their environment to more closely suit themselves. They may do this consciously, for who knows for certain whether they think or not, or what they think about? And they do, sometimes, somehow, grant wishes. For as I walked away, I passed a screening copse of pines. I turned and saw, not thirty feet away, a mature live oak, the same shape, the same size, as Old Grandfather.

I saw Old Grandfather in his prime.

About the Author

The Lonesome Hillbilly is a wanderer from birth. Born in the Lone Star Republic (but not in Texas), he traveled a thousand miles by his first birthday, and ten thousand by his second. He lives on a motorcycle, and in a tent he made. He has been in every state of the Union, plus Asia and Europe. Politically he

is a Rational Anarchist. Spiritually, he respects all religions, and no churches. He winters in the low deserts of Arizona, and tours all New Mexico during the Spring. The rest of the time, you will find him somewhere within five hundred miles of the Rocky Mountains. Probably.

Stay Free!